The Walt Disney World Challenge

Trivia Games, Quests, and Feats of Fancy in the Most Magical Place on Earth

William Bragg

Theme Park Press
The Happiest Books on Earth
www.ThemeParkPress.com

© 2018 William Bragg

No part of this publication may be reproduced, distributed, or transmitted in any form or by any means, including photocopying, recording, or other electronic or mechanical methods, without the prior written permission of the publisher, except for brief quotations embodied in critical reviews and certain other non-commercial uses permitted by copyright law.

Although every precaution has been taken to verify the accuracy of the information contained herein, no responsibility is assumed for any errors or omissions, and no liability is assumed for damages that may result from the use of this information.

Theme Park Press is not associated with the Walt Disney Company.

The views expressed in this book are those of the author and do not necessarily reflect the views of Theme Park Press.

Theme Park Press publishes its books in a variety of print and electronic formats. Some content that appears in one format may not appear in another.

Editor: Bob McLain
Layout: Artisanal Text

ISBN 978-1-68390-122-8
Printed in the United States of America

Theme Park Press | www.ThemeParkPress.com
Address queries to bob@themeparkpress.com

Contents

How to Use This Book v

Magic Kingdom 1
   Arrival 1
   Main Street, U.S.A. 2
   Adventureland 8
   Frontierland 15
   Liberty Square 22
   Fantasyland 28
   Tomorrowland 42
   Extra Magic 50

Epcot 53
   Future World East 53
   Future World West 56
   World Showcase 64

Hollywood Studios 81
   Hollywood Boulevard 81
   Echo Lake 82
   Grand Avenue 86
   Pixar Place 88
   Animation Courtyard 89
   Commissary Lane 91
   Sunset Boulevard 92

Animal Kingdom 99
   Oasis 99
   Discovery Island 100
   Africa 102
   Rafiki's Planet Watch 106

Asia 108
DinoLand U.S.A 113
Pandora: The World of Avatar 116

Walt Disney World Special Events   121
Walt Disney World Resort Challenge   127
Walt Disney World Snack Challenge   141
Disney Springs Challenge   143
Disney Character Challenge   147
Quiz Answers   153

About the Author   161
About Theme Park Press   163

How to Use This Book

This book can be used in many different ways:
- Use it as a tracker of all the different experiences at the theme parks, resorts, water parks, special events, and dining experiences at Walt Disney World that you have been completed at least once.
- Use it as a book to challenge family and friends a trip to Disney World.
- Use it as an informational guide to the hidden (or not-so-hidden) joys and secrets that can be found in the theme parks.
- Use it as an idea generator for different things to do at Disney World.
- Most importantly, use it to enhance your Disney World experience.

Each challenge is worth one point, and any challenge that has a bonus point associated with it is also worth one point (unless it offers a double bonus—then give yourself two points).

There are also quiz challenges spread throughout the four theme park sections, with answers in the back of the book.

As Walt Disney said: "The way to get started is to quit talking and begin doing."

So let's get started!

Magic Kingdom

ARRIVAL

MK1: There are multiple ways to get to the main entrance of the Magic Kingdom: ferryboats and the monorail from the Transportation and Ticket Center (TTC), bus from the resorts, or a nice leisurely stroll from the Contemporary. Take at least two of the four methods to get to the front gate (the tram from the parking lot to the TTC does not count).

MK2: Help a family with a stroller get on a tram. If you just happen to be that family with the stroller, then this challenge has been satisfied.

MK3: Try to ride on all three ferryboats: *Richard F. Irvine*, *Admiral Joe Fowler*, *General Joe Potter*.

MK4: Congratulations, you've survived the trains, planes, and automobiles to get to the gates of the Magic Kingdom. Your next challenge, should you choose to accept it: compliment the security guards on the fine work they are doing. Take a deep breath if the wait is long.

MK5: Finally, yes, through the gates. The Mickey bulb has lit green and you are stepping into the Magic Kingdom. Play tourist for a few minutes and get your picture taken with the floral Mickey face before proceeding.

MK6: As you head through the tunnel to your left or to your right, check out the "Coming Attraction" posters of various rides that you can experience while in the park. Bonus points if you get a whiff of popcorn cooking—like what you would experience in the lobby of a movie theater—just past the entrance to the tunnel.

MK7: The show is about to begin. Take a look down at the ground and note the color of the concrete. Notice how it changes color from gray to red. The show has begun. You are now walking the red carpet to the greatest show on earth. Welcome to Main Street, U.S.A.

MAIN STREET, U.S.A.

MK8: Are you celebrating something special (birthday, anniversary, first visit, whatever)? Pick up a button at Guest Relations in City Hall, but be prepared to have your celebration recognized throughout the day by cast members and often by other guests as well.

MK9: Speaking of which…recognize a fellow guest's special celebration pin and give them a nice greeting.

MK10: Head over to the Firehouse and pick up a Sorcerers of the Magic Kingdom map and "key card." You get one free set of cards per day. Bonus points for defeating all the villains.

MK11: Sunscreen, check; sunglasses, check; hat, oops. Find the Chapeau and pick out a hat for the day (or for the entire trip). Bonus points if you get it monogrammed with your name on it. Extra bonus points if you decide to go old school and get some mouse ears.

MK12: Take a deep dive into the Magic Kingdom with a "behind-the-scenes" tour of the park (there is an additional cost in addition to your park ticket). All the tours will be educational, but if you want to hit the backstage area and the Utilidor tunnels, consider Keys to the Kingdom tour.

MAGIC KINGDOM 3

Fun Fact: The Magic Kingdom has a whole Utilidor system underneath the park. It allows cast members and characters to move from one part of the park to another without interrupting the magic (as would happen if, say, a Jungle Cruise skipper were seen strolling through Tomorrowland).

MK13: Venture up the stairs to the Walt Disney World Railroad station. Look straight down Main Street toward Cinderella Castle. Notice how the use of forced perspective makes the castle look taller.

MK14: Take a ride around the park (it's about twenty minutes) on the Walt Disney World Railroad. Enjoy the scenery and plan your day. Bonus points if you ride on more than one of the four trains: the *Walter E. Disney*, the *Lilly Belle* (named after Walt's wife), the *Roger E. Broggie* (Walt's first Imagineer), and the *Roy O. Disney* (Walt's brother and business partner).

Fun Fact: The locomotives were pulled from a railroad boneyard in Mexico and restored in Florida.

MK15: Find a penny, pick it up, then all day, you'll have good luck...or at least a penny to try out the Mutascope. Go old school for your entertainment, and invest a penny to enjoy the earliest versions of motion pictures while you wait to board a train.

MK16: It's not often that you get an opportunity to meet a "talking" Mickey Mouse. Head over to the Town Square Theater for a unique character meet-and-greet. Swap some dialogue with the main mouse. Bonus points if you meet Tinker Bell in the same visit (and if you're the first in line to meet Tink, you get to wake her up).

MK17: Check out Town Square Exposition Hall. Notice that this building, compared to those around it, does not use the forced perspective technique that is dominant among the buildings found on Main Street?

Fun Fact: Disney Imagineers needed to block the Contemporary Resort from guests' view when they were standing in the turn-of-the-last-century atmosphere of Main Street.

MK18: Are you a *Lady and the Tramp* fan? Find their paw prints outlined by a heart in the pavement outside Tony's Town Square restaurant. Bonus points if you go inside and share some spaghetti with someone you love.

MK19: Find the Goofy statue in front of Tony's. Take a moment to sit down and listen carefully. You may be able to hear Goofy talking to you.

MK20: Feeling patriotic? Report to the Town Square's municipal park for the daily flag retreat at 1700 (5 p.m.). If you are a veteran, you can volunteer to serve as the veteran of the day during the flag-lowering ceremony. Inquire at City Hall, but do it early in the day (add bonus points if you are selected).

MK21: Still feeling patriotic? Be on the lookout for all the "American" flags on the buildings up and down Main Street. Patriotic, yes, but the flag poles serve as lightning rods. Bonus points if you can determine what is wrong with each flag that you find (for example, one less star, one less stripe).

Fun Fact: The faux flags are used so they don't have to be taken down at night (or illuminated).

MK22: Shave and a haircut...two bits. Drop into the Harmony Barber Shop to get a haircut or to just check out the nostalgic shaving items (for sale, of course).

MK23: Catch the Dapper Dans barbershop quartet performing live on Main Street. Bonus points if you sing along (but only in your head, okay).

MAGIC KINGDOM

MK24: Enjoy a turn of the-last-century mode of transportation to travel up or down Main Street: a horseless carriage, an early fire engine, a jitney, or a horse-drawn trolley. Bonus points if you get a ride with the Dapper Dans while they sing.

MK25: Take a picture with the cigar store Indian. If you bring children every year (or every couple of years), this is a good way to track growth. Bonus points if you find the cigar store Indian's twin in Frontierland.

Fun Fact: The Magic Kingdom used to have a shop called the Tobacconist which sold tobacco products. Since 2000, no tobacco products are sold in the theme parks.

MK26: Character meet-and-greets can be fast and furious here. Be on the lookout for your first character of the day; or, if you're on your way out, your last.

MK27: Main Street is often busy, but usually it is busiest during the early morning, during the parades, and after the fireworks at the end of the day. Step away from the action of the park in the middle of the day to explore the intricacies of Main Street.

MK28: Discover the Emporium window displays. Note the story that is being told in the windows as you make your way down the street.

Fun Fact: The windows of the Emporium are lower than normal so that children can see the displays.

MK29: Ever hear of a telephone party line? Find the antique-looking wall-mounted phone (the type with an ear piece that is separate from the mouth piece) in one of the stores along Main Street. Pick it up and listen to the conversation.

MK30: Indulge yourself, but you get to choose...either visit the Plaza Ice Cream Parlor or the Main Street

Confectionery to experience some nostalgia, and/or check out the Main Street Bakery to pick up some Starbucks coffee or baked goods. Bonus points if you can spot a Smellitizer.

Fun Fact: That smell of "just-out-of-the-oven" cookies isn't a coincidence. Walt Disney believed in engulfing his guests in all five senses. With smell being a strong trigger for memories, his Imagineers were sure to incorporate smells throughout the park. The process even has a name: Air Smellitizers.

MK31: Time to go old school. Get a silhouette of your head done on Main Street. Bonus points if you get it framed and hang it proudly when you get home.

MK32: If you don't want to eat a treat, you can still head into the Main Street Confectionery and watch the cast members create the sweet concoctions. Bonus points if you score a free sample.

MK33: Play ball. Hit up Casey's Corner and find out why there is no joy in Mudville ever since Mighty Casey struck out. Why you're at it, have a hot dog and enjoy the sounds of some great ragtime tunes.

Fun Fact: Walt Disney made a short called Casey at the Bat *in 1946.*

MK34: Walk down the middle of Main Street and take a picture with the castle as your background (individual or as a group). You can often find a cast member about 2/3 of the way down Main Street who will take your picture—either with your camera or theirs, or both.

MK35: Introduce yourself to one of the Citizens of Main Street, such as Mayor Weaver, reporter Scoop Sanderson, socialite Victoria Trumpetto, and Smokey Miller, the fire chief. You'll know them by their sashes. Bonus points if you cast a vote for the mayor in the previous election (make sure to let him know).

MAGIC KINGDOM

MK36: "76 Trombones" led the big parade. Catch the Main Street Philharmonic marching down the street. Bonus points if you dance to the music as you walk behind the band.

MK37: If Main Street is closed due to a parade or other event, and the streets are curb to wall with people, make your way from one end of the street to the other by walking through Emporium. Bonus points if you don't stop to buy anything.

MK38: Take a picture with the *Partners* statue in the central hub. Bonus points if you get some snapshots of one of the miniature statues surrounding the *Partners*.

Fun Fact: The statue is just about six-and-a-half-feet tall, but Walt Disney was only five feet ten inches.

MK39: Take a picture at the *Sharing the Magic* statue with Roy Disney and Minnie Mouse on a park bench.

MK40: Take a break from the hustle and the bustle and enjoy a rest on one of the many "Disney green" benches that line the end of Main Street. Bonus points if you can name a couple of the songs that are playing while you rest.

MK41: Stick around just past closing time (about 30 minutes) and watch the "Kiss Goodnight" show that is displayed on Cinderella Castle.

MK42: Find the Main Street window that reads: Elias Disney—Contractor—Est 1895. (It honors Walt and Roy Disney's father.)

MK43: Find the Main Street window that reads:The Big Wheel Co.—Horseless Carriages—Bob Gurr. (Gurr designed ride vehicles for such Disneyland attractions as Autopia, Haunted Mansion, the monorail, the Matterhorn Bobsleds, and the Submarine Voyage.)

MK44: Find the Main Street window that reads: General Joe's Building Permits Licensed in Florida—Gen. Joe Potter, Raconteur. (Potter helped build Disney World's underground utilities and infrastructure.)

MK45: Find the Main Street window that reads: Seven Summits Expeditions—Frank G. Wells, President, "For Those That Want to Do It All." (Wells was a former Disney executive and mountain climber who died in an helicopter accident while on a ski vacation).

MK46: Prior to the official park opening time, make your way to the stage in front of Cinderella Castle to experience trumpets and other royal fanfare as Mickey Mouse (along with a few friends) greets the day's visitors.

ADVENTURELAND

MK47: Seek out the most popular snack on property—Dole Whip—at Aloha Isle. Bonus points if you tackle the Citrus Swirl at the Sunshine Terrace during the same day.

MK48: The prodigal bird returns. Find the Orange Bird in Adventureland.

Fun Fact: The Orange Bird was a park icon created by the Florida Citrus Commission. He even had his own album (with singer Anita Bryant). The Orange Bird was removed from the parks in 1987, but returned as a fan favorite in 2012.

MK49: Channel your inner Aladdin or Jasmine and explore Agrabah Bazaar. Bonus points if you try on a fez hat.

MK50: Venture with Captain Jack Sparrow and a series of maps in your effort to gain control of the high seas. Bonus points if you complete your quest.

MAGIC KINGDOM

MK51: It's a pirate's life for me. If you have little ones in your party, head to the Pirates League and get them transformed into a pirate, a mermaid, or an empress. Bonus points if an adult does it with them.

MK52: Bring your appetite and your funny bone to the Skipper Canteen and see what Alberta Falls (she's the daughter of Albert Falls from the Jungle Cruise) has to offer. Bonus points if you finish off your meal by pleasing your sweet tooth with a Kungaloosh.

MK53: Pick up a magic talisman at the Crow's Nest and defeat Captain Barbossa and other enemies while completing different maps in "A Pirate's Adventure." Bonus points if you complete all five missions. Be sure you turn in your card to a cast member—you'll get a special something signed by Captain Jack.

Swiss Family Treehouse

MK54: No rest for the weary. Climb all 116 steps to the top of the treehouse.

Fun fact: The top of the treehouse sits six stories in the air, and its foundation is sunk four stories deep.

MK55: Discover the various rooms and find the following items: clamshell sink, mahogany furniture, and hammock. Bonus points if you discover the name of the ship that the Robinsons were sailing on when they became shipwrecked. Hint: Focus on the ship's wheel when you find it.

MK56: Reach the summit and enjoy a 360-degree view of the Magic Kingdom. Bonus points if you spot a Jungle Cruise boat on its voyage.

MK57: In the movie, the Robinsons had to battle a band of pirates. Find the cannon that helped fend off the swashbucklers.

MK58: What's the rush? Read the plaques of the three sons with highlights from their journal as you wind your way up and down the treehouse.

MK59: Enjoy the shade for a bit and watch the intricate water-wheel system taking water from the stream to the top of the treehouse in bamboo buckets.

The Magic Carpets of Aladdin

MK60: Have some fun if it is hot and enjoy a little camel "spit" to cool you off before/during/after (or all three) you take your magical ride. Bonus points if you recognize the camels from an earlier Aladdin parade (held at Disney-MGM Studios, now Disney's Hollywood Studios).

MK61: Control your elevation. Take flight in the front row and control how high or low you fly. Bonus points if you also try out the back row (tip your flying carpet forward or backward).

MK62: It's a whole new world. Unlock the Cave of Wonders by finding the scarab on the attraction.

MK63: Ask the guests in the carpet in front of you to take a photograph of you in flight (or preflight). Bonus points if you return the favor for the carpet in front or behind you.

Walt Disney's Enchanted Tiki Room

MK64: Spare a couple extra minutes and catch the pre-show. Check out the foliage, reminiscent of the Polynesian islands, while you wait.

MK65: Take a break from walking/standing, and the heat, and enjoy the fifteen-minute presentation. Bonus points if you catch the show while it is raining outside.

MAGIC KINGDOM

MK66: True or False. The thatched roof on the top of the Enchanted Tiki Room is actual vegetation that was grown at Disney to cover the attraction.

MK 67: Pay attention to Fritz, the German bird, and see if you can associate the voice with that of another famous celebrity from the animal world, Kellogg's Tony the Tiger.

MK68: Is that an accent I hear? Match the four main birds with their country of origin.

MK69: Warm up your vocal cords, and let it lose. Sing-along with the birds as they sing "In the Tiki, Tiki, Tiki, Tiki, Tiki, Room" or "Let's All sing Like The Birdies Sing." Bonus points if you sing along with both.

MK70: Don't rush out. Stop and check out a couple of the totem poles and Tiki drummers before you return to the Florida heat. Bonus points if you sing "Heigh-Ho" along with the Audio-Animatronics on your way out.

Jungle Cruise

MK71: Don't wait until the skipper starts with the humor; the jokes start in the queue. Find at least two jokes or name puns as you wind your way to your boat. Bonus points if you catch the shout out to E.L. O'Fevre (say it loud fast).

MK72: Find the crate bearing the company name of "Evans Exotic Plant Exporters." Bonus points if you know what the address for the company represents. Double bonus points if you can decipher the zip code.

Fun fact: This crate is a shout-out to Imagineer Bill Evans who was responsible for landscaping both Disneyland and much of Walt Disney World.

MK73: Check out the skippers' meal menus before you board. Do you spot a trend?

MK74: Find the chalkboard that lists the names of guests who have gone missing (Ilene Dover). Bonus points if you come up with your own witty name.

MK75: Finally to the loading docks? Note the names of the different boats as they come into the docks (each will highlight a major river found around the world).

MK76: Spot the beached plane during your tour of the jungle (there's only half a plane). Bonus points if you can name where the other half of the plane used to be located in a Disney theme park.

MK77: Find the Hidden Minnie as you venture through the temple. Hint: Look to the left side of the boat near the exit to the temple.

MK78: Name the four rivers (found throughout the world) that are represented on your expedition.

MK79: Find the backside of water!

MK80: Live it up a little and help your skipper. Use your own finger gun to fend off the angry hippos. Bonus points if you make a shooting sound when you fire your finger (pew! pew!).

MK81: As you are ducking the spears and arrows being sent across your boat when you come across the natives, listen carefully to what one of the natives is saying. If you hear "I love disco," you've earned the points.

MK82: Feeling festive? Time your visit to the Magic Kingdom right (seasonally speaking) and check out the converted "Jingle" Cruise. Bonus points for recognizing the change to holiday puns.

MK83: Be even more adventurous and tackle the Jungle Cruise at night!

MK84: True or False. The boats on the Jungle Cruise are on a track?

Fun fact: The skippers can control the speed of their boat; top speed is 3.2 feet per second.

MK85: Half the fun (or most of it) of the cruise are the jokes and puns that the skippers rattle off in quick succession. Take the cruise twice to compare the jokes and puns. Bonus points if you can match them pun for pun (but do it in your head).

Pirates of the Caribbean

MK86: Catch the surprisingly familiar and pleasing smell of the seven seas on your voyage. Bonus points if you can match that smell to two other attractions found at Walt Disney World theme parks.

MK87: Take the longer standby route through the queue and find the cannons and ammunition stockpiles as you go deeper into the Castillo del Morro fortress.

MK88: If you venture off on to the FastPass+ side (fort side) of the queue, find the longest-running game of chess at the Magic Kingdom.

Fun fact: The board pieces are set up to replicate an actual stalemate (thus the reason the pirates are now skeletons).

MK89: Hold on to your hat, matey. Enjoy a refreshing plunge (in your boat) into a pirate attack on a Spanish stronghold in the Caribbean.

Fun fact: While the plunge adds to the excitement of your voyage, it is necessary due to the attraction's location. Boats must plummet down the waterfall to pass underneath the railroad tracks.

MK90: Find the skull and crossbones warning you that "Dead men tell no tales."

Fun fact: The white skull and crossbones on a black background is known as the Jolly Roger and became one of the more popular flag designs for pirate ships.

MK 91: Listen closely and compare the voice of the pirate auctioneer and your Ghost Host from the Haunted Mansion. Did you notice they are the same person (Paul Frees)? If so, give yourself the points.

MK92: Locate the helmsman in Dead Man's Cave. Bonus points if you catch him when some lightning is going off around him.

Fun fact: The helmsman was the inspiration behind the first movie poster for Pirates of the Caribbean: The Curse of the Black Pearl.

MK93: Sing along with the serenading pirates. If you don't know the words, just sing the "yo-ho" part.

MK94: We wants the red head! Place your bid when you sail through the auction scene.

MK95: After the auction, determine what the pirates are chasing around the room. Hint: Pay attention to what the women in the previous scene were holding.

Fun fact: This scene has changed quite often. First, the pirates chased the women, then the women chased the pirates, now the pirates chase....well, you'll figure it out.

MK96: Where's the captain? See if you can spot Captain Jack Sparrow all three times that he appears.

MK97: Cannonball! Sail through the battle scene without getting splashed by a wayward projectile almost hitting your ship.

Fun fact: Disney Imagineers use flashes of lights, air cannons, and underwater blast to bring the battle to life (no cannonballs are actually flying over your head).

MAGIC KINGDOM

MK98: True or False. In the scene where the city is in flames, is the fire is real?

Fun fact: When the Anaheim fire marshal reviewed the original Pirates of Caribbean at Disneyland, he believed that the fire was real.

MK99: Locate the dog holding the keys to the jail cell. Bonus points if you can get him to give you the keys.

MK100: As if the Audio Animatronics didn't seem real enough, examine the pirate on the bridge as you pass beneath him (this is the closest you get to one of the pirates). Notice the dirty feet and the hairy legs.

MK101: You've survived the plunge, the battle, and the fire, now it's time to survive the search for some pirate booty. Check out the pirate gift store. Bonus points if you have a little sword fight.

Fun fact: While it is common now, this was the first Magic Kingdom attraction that let out into a gift shop.

FRONTIERLAND

MK102: Pay attention as you move from Liberty Square into Frontierland. Note how you are moving from one part of America's history from its humble beginnings in the 1700s to the late 1800s once you enter Frontierland. Bonus points if you noticed that you are actually moving from east (Liberty Square, representing an eastern city) to west (St. Louis and beyond).

MK103: Listen carefully as you walk the trails of Frontierland. Take the points if you catch either *Cowboy's Lament*, *Ghost Riders in the Sky*, or *The Ballad of Davy Crockett*.

Fun fact: The Ballad of Davy Crockett was a multi-million dollar single produced by Disney.

MK104: Gather your family and friends and tell them to bring their appetite (between 3 and 6pm). Report to Pecos Bill Tall Tale Inn and Café and take the Nachos Rio Grande Challenge (it feeds about six to eight guests). Bonus points if you (with your group) finish the nachos before leaving Pecos Bill.

MK105: Hungry or not, snoop around and check out the Old West-themed memorabilia sprinkled throughout Pecos Bill. Bonus points for reading the story of Pecos Bill and finding at least two pieces of "tall tale" memorabilia/tributes (such as Slue Foot Sue's gloves or Paul Bunyan's axe).

MK106: Since Pecos Bill Tall Tale Inn and Café borders both Adventureland and Frontierland, find both entrances and note the differences in the signs overhead.

MK107: Try your hand with a .54-caliber Hawkins buffalo rifle at the Frontierland Shootin' Arcade. Bonus points if you take down over half of the targets modeled after Boot Hill in Tombstone, Arizona.

MK108: Enjoy a BBQ buffet at Diamond Horseshoe (modeled after a 1800s musical saloon).

Fun fact: This restaurant used to have the Diamond Horseshoe Revue, a show with can-can dancers, singers, a band, and a comedian.

MK109: All aboard! Catch a ride to Fantasyland or Main Street on the Walt Disney World Railroad out of the Frontierland station. Bonus points if you find the wooden leg named Smith (shout out to Mary Poppins).

Big Thunder Mountain Railroad

MK110: Welcome to the Wildest Ride in the Wilderness: Big Thunder Mountain. Ride this attraction at night and compare it to a daylight experience. Which did you like better? Bonus points if you ride while the fireworks are going off at night.

MK111: Everything has a backstory at Disney. While in line for Big Thunder Mountain, find the portrait of Barnabus T. Bullion, the founder and president of the Big Thunder Mining Company.

Fun Fact: The picture is actually Tony Baxter, the head Imagineer for the development of this attraction.

MK112: Find the pay scale listed in the Mining Office. Take the points if you notice anything funny about the foreman's name.

MK113: Looking to cause a little extra chaos for mine train travelers? Find the dynamite plungers and/or wheel cranks and give them a push or a spin. They will set off the explosions (water, steam, noise) that the trains experience.

MK114: Safety is paramount, especially when mining. Stop and check the "AutoCanary" machine to see if the canary is alive. Bonus points if you can smell what the canary is smelling.

Fun fact: In Disney's Enchanted Tiki Room, Jose wonders what happened to Rosita. The canary cage in the ventilation room is labeled "Rosita."

MK115: Stop and smell the roses, or in this case, stop in the queue and take a look into Mine Shaft 7 at the Performance Post.

MK116: It's not often you get to check out animals while you're riding a run-away roller coaster. Count the number of different types of animals that you find throughout your journey on Big Thunder Mountain (and yes, the dinosaur bones count).

MK117: Watch one of the mine workers' "home movies."

MK118: If you are riding the railroad at night, pay attention to the saloon when you ride by it. Give yourself the points if you catch the shadows of the townspeople having a party.

MK119: True or False. Big Thunder Mountain is faster than Space Mountain.

MK120: Do some exploring. Find real antique mining equipment throughout the site. Bonus points if you find the old ball mill that was used to pull gold from ore.

MK121: Find the miner taking a bath.

MK122: Ask to sit in the very back of the mine train. The view is better, you have more time to take everything in, and it feels like you are going faster.

MK123: Before you venture into the mines, check out the various names of the railroad locomotives that you are about to board.

Country Bear Jamboree

MK124: Escape the heat and duck into Grizzly Hall, but before you do, see if you can spot the bear skin rugs adorning the second-story walls by the entrance. Bonus point if you score yourself a dessert next door before you go into the pre-show area.

MK125: Welcome your master of ceremonies: Henry. Count the number of different stages that Henry appears on. If you counted three, take the points.

MK126: Welcome Melvin, Buff, and Max. While you are enjoying their heckling, determine which one is a bit dim-witted, which one is the leader, and which one is just happy to be there.

MK127: Which famous country singer and actor is the voice of Henry and Max?

MK128: Find the only bear that is not sporting any clothes. Hint: He is usually highlighted at the end of a group number, and his teddy bear squeaks.

MK129: Not many musicians can pull off playing a corn jug. Locate two of the three jugs that "Ted" has at his disposal during the group musical numbers (he's holding a B-flat jug).

Fun fact: The country-western group is called the Five Bear Rugs.

MK130: Listen carefully when Trixie hits the stage. Where does Henry (her crush) say that she hails from?

Fun fact: Trixie is voiced by Cheryl Pool who was voted Top New Female Vocalist by the Academy of Country Music in 1968.

MK131: Pick a favorite to complete this challenge: Teddy Barra's "Heart, We Did All That We Could versus Big Al's "Blood on the Saddle." Bonus points if you can sing along with either one of them.

MK132: Spot Sammy the raccoon throughout the show. Hint: Check out Henry's coonskin hat (fitting when they are singing "The Ballad of Davy Crockett."

MK133: All good things must come to an end. Clap and sing (or just clap) with the crew as they drive Big Al off the stage.

Splash Mountain

MK134: While waiting to board your log flume, find the shadow of Br'er Toad relaxing in a rocking chair. Did you hear him singing?

MK 135: Once you approach the loading area, find the flashing lantern and follow the pattern. Did you notice that it flashes when the logs are ready to move? If so, give yourself the points.

MK136: Locate all three of the Br'ers: Br'er Bear, Br'er Fox, and Br'er Rabbit.

MK137: Find the gopher on your voyage (he comes out of the ceiling) and listen carefully to what he is saying. If you pick up the F-S-U chant, give yourself the challenge points.

Fun fact: FSU refers to Florida State University, the alma mater of one of the Disney Imagineers.

MK138: You aren't just in for one large drop. Count the number of gut-wrenching drops that occur throughout your adventure. If you capture all three, give yourself the points.

MK139: *Song of the South* was known for its catchy tunes. Sing along with characters and catch at least two of the three songs played in Splash Mountain: "Zip-a-Dee-Doo-Dah," Ev'rybody's Got a Laughing Place," and "How Do You Do." Bonus points if you sing and clap your hands along with characters on the riverboat.

MK140: Speaking of characters. Splash Mountain is full of critters. Find at least eight different animal species on your journey.

MK141: Smile for the birdie. About half a second into your drop, Disney will capture your ride experience. Make your picture memorable and coordinate with your fellow log flume riders. Bonus points if you take a picture of the camera taking a picture of you and you get a picture of the screen after the ride. Sounds confusing, but it's not.

MK142: Take the 52-foot fall in your log flume like a champ—arms up and screaming. Bonus points if you don't get wet. Those sitting in the front of the log flume have a tendency to get drenched more than those in the back.

MK143: You've tried it in the day time, now try it at night. If you time it just right, you can see the fireworks as you plummet back to earth.

MK144: Didn't get wet enough on the attraction? Hang out on the bridge in front of the flume drop and wait for the water cannon to spray the bridge (it happens every third log flume). Bonus points if you talk someone into waiting on the bridge and they get sprayed.

MK145: Got a little critter in your group? Take a break and watch them yuck it up at the Laughin' Place, a special area for kids that do not meet the 40-inch height requirement for Splash Mountain.

Tom Sawyer Island

MK146: True or False. The log rafts run along a track to get you safely across the Rivers of America and to the island.

Fun fact: The rafts are powered by natural-gas motors.

MK147: Everything has a theme...even your rafts. Find the different names for the rafts (they are all taken from characters Mark Twain's *Adventures of Tom Sawyer*).

MK148: Make yourself at home. Play a game of checkers while you're on the island. Bonus points if you win.

MK149: Put on your explorer hat. Brave Injun Joe's Cave from start to finish (even the dark narrow passageways).

MK150: Make your way to Harper's Mill to check out the giant waterwheel, but listen carefully. Give yourself the points if you can hear the mill pump out the melody of "Down by the Old Mill Stream."

Fun fact: The mill is a shout out to the early Disney animated short The Old Mill. Look closely for a little blue bird sitting between the cogs (just like in the film).

MK151: Take a rest break at Aunt Polly's front porch. Bonus points if you brought your lunch to eat it here (or at the park benches near Scavenger's Fort). More bonus points if you capture a unique picture of the Haunted Mansion across the Rivers of America or the steamboat as it passes.

MK152: If you have a little one (12 or under), head to playground at Tom Sawyer's Scavenger Fort.

MK153: Hop, bounce, jump, or hold on for dear life as you cross the barrel bridge (don't worry, it's safe). Bonus points if you don't have to hold on to the sides with both hands.

MK154: Explore Fort Langhorn and be sure to check out the guns in the Rifle Roost (fire at the Big Thunder mine trains if you get a chance).

Fun fact: The fort is named after Mark Twain. It was his middle name when he was known as Samuel Langhorne Clemens (they removed the "e" from the fort's name).

LIBERTY SQUARE

MK155: Check out Columbia Harbour House. If you noticed it is sporting two distinct themes, give yourself the points

Fun fact: Columbia Harbour House is themed after Europe the closer you are to Fantasyland, but as you progress

through the restaurant toward Liberty Square, the theming transforms to early American.

MK156: Find the animals on the Columbia Harbour House sign.

Fun fact: In colonial days, many people did not know how to read, so restaurants would place animals on their sign to indicate what kind of food was served there.

MK157: Examine the exterior of the buildings. Pay close attention to the shutters. Did you notice anything different about how they are hung? If you answered yes, they are at an angle. Take the points.

Fun fact: During the Revolutionary War, leather straps were used to hang the shutters because there was no metal being shipped from England, so the colonists used the metal in the shutters to make ammunition and replaced it with leather straps.

MK158: Look at the walkways in Liberty Square and find the difference in pavement colors. Bonus points if you can figure out why there is a different color paving throughout this land (ask a cast member if you can't).

MK159: Find the Liberty Tree and count the number of lanterns adorning it.

Fun fact: The tree is over 130 years old and weighs in excess of 35-tons.

MK160: "Listen, my children, and you shall hear, the midnight ride of Paul Revere." Find the replica of the House of Burgesses and the two lanterns hanging in an upstairs window ("two if by sea").

MK161: Find the Liberty Bell replica—no ringing it, though.

The Haunted Mansion

MK162: Catch the Haunted Mansion when the wait time is listed as 13 minutes. Why? That means there is no wait to enter.

MK163: Skip the Fast Pass+ for the Haunted Mansion and play with the interactive queue. Bonus points if the eyes on Madame Leota's tombstone open and stare at you.

MK164: Find the ghost horse pulling the carriage, but don't try to feed it any carrots or sugar cubes. Bonus points if you follow the hoof prints to the stable.

MK165: In the queue, be on the lookout for the multiple tributes on the tombstone surrounding the Haunted Mansion. Some are even named after Disney Imagineers (see if you can pick any out that you might have also found on the windows on Main Street).

MK166: See if you can get one of the Haunted Mansion cast members to crack a smile. They aren't supposed to break character.

MK167: As you listen carefully to your ghost host, determine whether the walls are stretching up or down. Pick out a favorite morbid portrait while you're at it.

Fun Fact: The Magic Kingdom's stretching room moves up, whereas the stretching room in Disneyland's Haunted Mansion moves down.

MK168: Meet your Ghost Host during the final portion of the stretching room scene. Don't "hang" around too long. Find the portrait of the Ghost Host before he became part of the 999 happy haunts. Hint: Look for a man with an axe and a noose around his neck.

MK169: During the attic scene, count the number of grooms that the axe-wielding bride has taken. If you counted five and made it out alive, you've survived the challenge. Bonus points if you noticed that she's wearing an extra set of pearls in each portrait.

MK170: During the stretching room scene, locate Constance (she's the one holding a rose) and her husband George (he's the one with a very stout moustache and an axe in his head). Locate them once again during the ride (it will be in a portrait: she'll have a rose, and he will be sporting the same moustache, though minus the axe). Give yourself double the points if you win this matching game.

MK171: Quoth the raven: "Nevermore." As a shout out to Edgar Allen Poe, find at least two ravens as you venture through the gothic manor.

Fun fact: In the early design of the attraction, the raven actually had narration.

MK172: During the Haunted Mansion's Great Hall scene, determine what is so unique about the waltzing ghost couples. Hint: Who is leading who? Ask a cast member if you can't figure it out.

MK173: Listen closely to Madame Leota as you ride your Doom Buggy through her séance room in the Haunted Mansion. Name a couple of Disney characters that were also voiced by the talented Eleanor Audley. Hint: Think stepmom and envious dragons.

MK174: Be on the lookout for hitch-hiking ghosts trying to break free of the Haunted Mansion. Phineas carries the carpet bag, Gus has the ball and chain, and Ezra is tall and gangly. Your challenge is to experience all three ghosts, but you score points for each.

MK175: Just to see if it is any different (since the ride is dark anyway), ride the Haunted Mansion after the sun goes down, too.

MK176: Find and check out the pet cemetery. Bonus points if you locate J. Thaddeus Toad's tombstone. It's a shout out to the retired Mr. Toad's Wild Ride (replaced by Winnie the Pooh).

Fun fact: The cemetery was designed by Kim Irvine, daughter of Imagineer Leota Toombs (aka Madame Leota).

MK177: Drop by Momento Mori and check out the goodies for sale there. Bonus points if you get a holographic haunted photo of yourself.

The Hall of Presidents

MK178: Look up at the address before you enter the hall and determine what historical event the numbers represent. Hint: The event took place in Philadelphia at Independence Hall.

MK179: Want to see the presidential seal without going to Washington D.C.? Duck inside the Hall of Presidents and find it.

Fun fact: It took an act of Congress for the Magic Kingdom to be allowed to use the seal.

MK180: Arrive before the show and explore the museum-like lobby. Find at least two dresses worn by former First Ladies.

MK181: There is a plethora of articles previously owned by past presidents. Take a look around before the show and find at least three.

MK182: The film captures many of the difficulties that America faced during its formative years. Who is providing the narration for the film?

MK183: Think back to your Civil War history lessons. Attempt to recite as much of the Gettysburg Address as you can when the Audio-Animatronic Abraham

Lincoln delivers the speech (it's only 272 words). Bonus points if you know how many years four score and seven years ago equals.

Fun fact: The precursor to this show, Great Moments with Mr. Lincoln, was developed for the state of Illinois by Walt Disney for the 1964 New York World's Fair. This show currently runs at Disneyland.

MK184: Pay close attention to all the presidents as they are being introduced, and take the points if you noticed that each of them is wearing authentic reproductions of clothing from their era.

MK185: No detail is too small for Disney. When Franklin Delano Roosevelt is introduced, figure out what is particularly unique about him. Focus on his legs (and remember your history lessons).

Liberty Square Riverboat

MK186: Explore all three levels of the *Liberty Belle* that are open to guests (the promenade deck, the Texas (or sun) deck, and the main deck).

MK187: During your tour, spot four of the main attractions surrounding the Rivers of America (Big Thunder Mountain, Splash Mountain, Tom Sawyer Island, and the Haunted Mansion).

MK188: Get your camera ready. Snap a shot of the Liberty Square riverboat as it cruises the waterways. Bonus points if you catch it at night when it is lit up.

MK189: True or False: The Liberty Square riverboat is a fully functioning steamboat that does not run on a track.

MK190: Locate any type of wildlife hanging out on Tom Sawyer Island while you are riding the riverboat.

MK191: While enjoying your journey, venture to the stern (rear of the ship) and watch the powerful paddle wheel plow through the Rivers of America.

MK192: The captain of the *Liberty Belle* selects a family to accompany him to the pilothouse on the top deck. Your challenge: be that family and help pilot the riverboat around the Rivers of America. Bonus points if you get to sound the whistle or ring the bell.

MK193: Make time for ice cream. Attend Tiana's Riverboat Party and Ice Cream Social and watch the parade afterwards from the riverboat. Bonus points if you meet Princess Tiana and Prince Naveen.

FANTASYLAND

MK194: Visit Castle Couture and find Aurora. Notice anything incredible about her dress? Think back to the end of Sleeping Beauty (pink dress, no blue dress, no pink dress). Bonus points if you ask a cast member serving in Castle Couture for some pixie dust.

MK195: Pressed penny memory time (one of the least expensive collector items in the parks). Head into Castle Couture and have a pressed penny made of either Tiana, Aurora, or Rapunzel. Bonus points if you get all three.

MK196: In front of the Prince Charming Regal Carrousel is Sword in the Stone. Pick your mightiest warrior (or your weakest) to give the sword a pull to try to remove it from the stone. Bonus points if someone from your group becomes the next king of England.

MK197: Wait until dusk and make your way over to the Tangled themed rest area. While you're enjoying the lighting of the lanterns, find at least three of the hidden Pascals.

Fun fact: The Tangled rest area used to be the Fantasyland loading/unloading dock for the Magic Skyway (gondola ride) which closed in 1999.

MK198: Check out the Pinocchio Village Haus restaurant and find four of the seven Pinocchio-themed rooms. Bonus points if you catch sight of a boat departing on the "it's a small world" cruise.

Cinderella Castle

MK199: Go behind the castle and look for a water fountain in front of the statue of Cinderella (before she was a princess). When you bend over to take a drink, take a look at the statue. Is the crown in the backdrop sitting on top of Cinderella's head?

MK200: Get selected to stay in Cinderella Castle for the night. (If you complete this challenge, turn in your challenge book...you've already won it all!)

MK201: Didn't get selected for a night in the Royal Suite? That's all right. Find the area of the castle (from the ground level; please don't go searching for the elevator) in which the special suite resides. Hint: Take a look up from the Fantasyland side and find the three clustered stained glass windows.

MK202: Find the glass mosaic inside Cinderella Castle. Take a look at the eyes of the step sisters: green tile for envy and red tile for anger.

MK203: Time for some Pixie Dust. Capture Tinker Bell flying out of the castle to the Tomorrowland Terrace.

MK204: Find the clock on Cinderella Castle. Notice anything funny/odd about one of the Roman numerals? If you found the IIII, give yourself the points, but this is actually correct. The Roman numeral IV wasn't used until post-colonial times. Bonus points if you find the clock in the stained glass of the castle suite and figure out how the Roman numeral four is betrayed there.

MK205: Beat the tourist trap picture from the front of the castle at the end of Main Street, U.S.A. Venture to the Liberty Square bridge and snap a family photo with the castle and the moat highlighted in the background.

MK206: True or False. The drawbridge cannot be raised like the bridge at Sleeping Beauty Castle at Disneyland?

MK207: Determine if forced perspective was used while building the castle, and if so, what gives it away?

MK208: Pamper yourself and meet a Disney princess or two. Dine at Cinderella's Royal Table. Bonus points if you dine before park opening and you get to walk down Main Street with no one else around.

MK209: Have a little princess in your group? Splurge and let her channel her inner princess at the Bibbidi Bobbidi Boutique (boys can be transformed into valiant knights). No princesses or knights? Peek in and check out the boutique and watch the transformations take place.

Prince Charming Regal Carrousel

MK210: Familiarize yourself with the story of Cinderella while in the queue. Check out the eighteen vignettes adorning the panels above the hand-carved stallions.

MK211: Get in the theme of things. Practice your best jousting moves as you ride your noble steed.

Fun fact: Disney Imagineers constructed a backstory of Prince Charming using the carrousel as a training device for jousting tournaments.

MAGIC KINGDOM 31

MK212: Rumor has it, you can ride Cinderella's very own horse. Find the horse, "Cindy," with the golden bow on its tail (no other horse has a tail ribbon) and mount that steed.

MK213: Pay close attention to the detail on your mount. Did you notice the 23-karat gold leaf that gives the horse a gilded appearance? If so, take the points. Bonus points if you found the real silver or bronze also.

Fun fact: The horses stay in pristine condition because every steed is refinished at least once every two years.

MK214: Enjoy more than two thousand glimmering lights and ride the carrousel in the evening.

Princess Fairytale Hall

MK215: There are two queues (one for Cinderella and a friend, one for Rapunzel and a "visiting" friend). Complete both queues to get the challenge points.

MK216: Find at least four portraits of Disney princesses in the queue.

MK217: Other than meeting a princess, the highlight is finding the famous glass slipper. Hint: Look for the purple pillow.

MK218: If you get to meet Rapunzel, ask her what her favorite book is. Bonus points if you ask her if Maximus and Flynn (Eugene) are getting along.

The Many Adventures of Winnie the Pooh

MK219: Have a little fun in Pooh queue. Crawl through a tunnel (your age doesn't matter). Be sure someone gets a picture, or it didn't happen. If you aren't that adventurous, try one of the other interactive activities

(Rabbit's Garden, Hunny Wall, Piglet's House). Bonus points if you do more than one.

MK220: Find the carving of the *Nautilus* (the submarine from *20,000 Leagues Under the Sea*) in the queue. Hint: Focus on the treehouse play area at the entrance to the attraction.

MK221: Catch the scent of honey as you travel through the attraction in your honey pot.

MK222: Match the illusion in Pooh's dream sequence with an attraction in Liberty Square.

MK223: Find the picture of Mr. Toad handing a deed over to Owl (focus on the walls in Owl's house). Bonus points if you also find the picture of Winnie the Pooh and Moley.

Fun fact: The Many Adventures of Winnie the Pooh replaced Mr. Toad's Wild Ride.

MK224: Your honey pot has a special design technique. Channel your best Tigger and figure out what motion-enhanced technique is used.

Mickey's PhilharMagic

MK225: While you are being wowed with the 3-D effects of the PhilharMagic, see if you catch the scent of apple and cinnamon as the pie floats in front of you.

MK226: On your magical music extravaganza, you are transported into five classic Disney settings. Place the setting with the movie and song that is represented.

MK227: Donald is explicitly told by Mickey not to wear Yesnid's (from *Fantasia*) hat, and of course he does just before everything goes haywire. Figure out the true meaning of the name Yesnid.

MK228: Find the mural that adorns the walls of the lobby and see how many musically themed Disney animated movies you can pick out. If you can name more than two, take the points.

Mad Tea Party

MK229: Your ride will only last 90 seconds. Take a few of those seconds to track your tea cup moving from one turntable to another (there are three in total). Bonus points if you can track your movement to each turntable.

MK230: You never know who you are going to run into at this attraction. Take a spin with Alice, the Mad Hatter, the White Rabbit, or the brothers Tweedle (Dee and Dum). Take the points if they are riding in any of the other 17 cups, but double the points if they are riding in yours.

MK231: Read the leaf-shaped plaque on the outer rim of the attraction (it has a quote from Randy Pausch, a former Imagineer and author of *The Last Lecture*).

MK232: Master the hand-over-hand spinning technique. Put all of your might into spinning your tea cup. Bonus points if you make someone move in their seat.

MK233: Go hands free and ride without any spinning.

MK234: Keep an eye for the dormouse (focus on the teapot in the middle). Catch the dormouse popping out of the teacup and take the points.

Peter Pan's Flight

MK235: Skip the FastPass+ line at least once and enjoy the new and improved interactive queue for Peter Pan's Flight. Review all of the portraits to refresh your memory of the story of Peter Pan.

MK236: Shadow dancing at its best. Play with the silhouetted objects on the screen that displays the shadows of guests, and interact with the items.

MK237: Find Tinker Bell spreading her pixie dust throughout the nursery. Bonus points if you catch her in lighting up the chest.

MK238: After being doused with pixie dust, allowing your ship to fly, find the building blocks by Wendy's bed, and decipher what they spell.

MK239: While flying over London in your pirate ship, take a look down and find the moving headlights that are mimicking cars moving through the bustling city.

Fun fact: Those headlights are really just tiny dots of blacklight paint on a continuously running bike chain.

MK240: While flying over Old London, find Big Ben.

Fun fact: Disney Imagineers used forced perspective while designing the buildings and streets of London to give guests the feeling that they are flying higher than they really are.

MK241: Peter Pan's Flight makes use of the omnimover system. Name another Magic Kingdom attraction that uses the same type system. Bonus points if you can determine the main difference between this one and the others.

MK242: Look closely and find Ariel from *The Little Mermaid* in the mermaid lagoon area of the attraction.

"it's a small world"

MK243: Sing-along time. You know you want to. Sing the song in its entirety from start to finish as you float through the attraction. Bonus points if you can sing along in another language.

Fun fact: The song is sung in five languages—English, Italian, Japanese, Spanish, and Swedish—and is continuously playing in at least two Disney theme parks around the world at all times.

MK244: Find the doll hanging off the Eiffel Tower.

Fun fact: This particular doll is made in the likeness of Imagineer Joyce Carlson who was in charge of costume and design for every version of the attraction throughout the world.

MK245: If you are wearing a MagicBand during your world tour, find your name highlighted during the final "goodbye" scene. Bonus points if you can say goodbye in more than three languages.

MK246: True or False. All of the dolls (with the exception of skin, clothes, eye/hair color) are the same throughout your voyage.

Fun fact: There are 289 dolls representing 29 countries.

MK247: Find the only two dolls that are representative of the United States: the Eskimo and the cowboy.

MK248: Only one country is called out by name. Find the reference to Mexico during your cruise. Hint: Look at the hats in the South American section.

MK249: "There is just one moon and one golden sun." There is one moon and one sun in every room. Locate them all to complete the challenge.

MK250: Find the Hidden Mickey in the Africa scene (think purple flowers).

MK251: There are several unique dolls. Find three of the five listed to complete this challenge: Tower of London guards, can-can dancers, Don Quixote, snake charmer, kite flyers.

Enchanted Forest

MK252: Visit Belle's Village and take in the detailed architecture of this quaint little provincial area.

MK253: Pick the most muscle-bound member of your party and have them size up for a photo op with Gaston's statue at the water fountain.

MK254: Locate the stunning chandelier made of nothing but horns and lights in Gaston's Tavern. Bonus points if you also locate his bow and arrows.

MK255: Drinking challenge for all ages. Give LeFou's Brew a go.

MK256: Practice a little French as you walk through Belle's Village. Greet at least one guest and one cast member with a hardy "bonjour."

MK257: No one meets-and-greets like Gaston. Either watch Gaston interact with other guests or meet him yourself. This is one that you don't want to miss. Bonus points if you challenge him to a push-up contest. Double bonus points if anyone in your group is dressed like Belle.

Seven Dwarfs Mine Train

MK258: There are plenty of woodland creatures in *Snow White*. Find the impressions in the ground left behind by the forest animals in the outdoor queue (there may even be some acorn impressions).

MK259: Heigh-ho, heigh-ho, it's off to work we go. Play the interactive jewel sorting game (be sure you follow Doc's note) or play the jewel-washing station and produce a melody from *Snow White* using the twelve spigots provided (each spigot represents a musical note). Bonus points if you play both of them.

MAGIC KINGDOM

MK260: You can have a barrel of fun while you wait. Once you enter the vaults, find the wooden barrel interactive game inside the vault and watch the ceiling overhead get transformed as you spin the barrels.

MK261: Shout out to Dopey. Find the key to the vault (focus on the entrance to the vault).

MK262: Find the vultures perched on the crane.

Fun fact: This is a shout-out to the vultures from the film and to those that had appeared in the Snow White's Scary Adventure attraction.

MK263: Check out the intricate details of the mine carts (focus on how no two carts are alike and the aging technique that was used by Disney Imagineers... all the way down to the bolts.

MK264: Hands up and eyes open as you venture through the Enchanted Forest in your mine cart. Catch the breathtaking view of Fantasyland when you reach the top of the first hill. Bonus points if you capture the view at night or during the fireworks.

MK265: The Disney Imagineers outdid themselves on the development of this attraction. Catch the independent movement of your mine train (compared to the cart in front of you). It swings side to side as you move along the rails. No two rides are alike!

MK266: Welcome to the jewel mine. There are six colored jewels in all: amber, blue, clear, green, purple, and red. Find all six to complete the challenge.

MK267: Home from work we go. You are done in the mines. Find the shadows of the dwarfs as they are marching out of the mine.

Fun fact: Disney Imagineers used a rotoscoping technique to display the dwarfs marching (just like they did in the movie).

MK268: Name all seven dwarfs. Bonus points if you can find each of them at least once during your ride.

MK269: Find the dwarfs dancing with Snow White at the end of the ride. (focus on the cottage as you are about to pull into the station). Bonus points if you catch sight of the Evil Queen.

Fun fact: Five of the dwarf figures in the cottage were once part of Snow White's Scary Adventure (Snow White, Dopey, and Sneezy are original).

MK270: Relive your Seven Dwarfs Mine Train adventure by purchasing a picture or a video of your journey. Bonus points if you had your hands up when they took your picture.

Under the Sea ~ Journey of the Little Mermaid

MK271: Check out the waterfalls, rugged cliffs, and serene waves. Find the shipwrecked vessel and the unique figurehead that adorns it.

MK272: While making your way through the queue (it must be during a certain time of the day), be on the lookout for a "shadow" Hidden Mickey that is created by the sunlight shining on hanging fabric.

MK273: Find the blue crabs in the Journey of the Little Mermaid queue and help them determine the difference between trash and treasure. Bonus points for sticking around and listening to Scuttle's explanations of items. You can never have too many dinglehoppers.

MK274: Board your clamshell and hold your breath. It's time to submerge into the briny deep ocean. Find at least three of Ariel's treasures in the "Part of Your World" scene.

MK275: Do your best Jamaican crab impression, and join Sebastian and the rest of the sea creatures in singing "Under the Sea." Bonus points if you perform a few conga line moves in your clamshell.

Fun fact: There are over 180 characters throughout your journey.

MK276: Find Jetsam and Floatsam in two different locations during the ride.

MK277: True or False. Ursula is one of the largest Audio-Animatronics in the Magic Kingdom.

MK278: Before you catch the bouquet, examine Ariel's wedding dress closely. Did you notice the embroidery and that the sequins are starfish and seahorses? If you did, take the points.

MK279: Stop by Ariel's Grotto for a meet-and-greet with Ariel in all of her mermaid splendor.

Enchanted Tales with Belle

MK280: Explore Maurice's cottage on your way to his workshop. Find the portrait of Belle (when she was younger) and her mother.

MK281: While in the workshop, study Maurice's workmanship and plans. Find three of these five objects to complete the challenge: sketches, drawing board, tools, two completed creations.

MK282: Behold the power of the Magic Mirror and prepare to meet Madame Wardrobe. Volunteer for a part in the re-enactment of the story and give it your all if you are assigned a speaking role. Bonus points if Lumière talks to you directly.

MK283: Even if you don't have a part, join the interactive experience. As an audience member, howl with the wind, ride the horse, or shiver in the dungeon to complete the challenge. No holding back.

MK284: You won't be able to get it out of your head for the rest of your day at the Magic Kingdom, but join in with the singing of "Be Our Guest." Bonus points if you leave with a bookmark from Belle.

MK285: True or False. In the library, guests will find over 12,000 books.

MK286: After the show, take a minute to meet with Belle. Bonus points if you offer her a rose.

Storybook Circus

MK287: Beat the heat. Take a run through Casey Jr. Soak 'N' Splash Station. By the way, you will get wet.

MK288: Check out the Relaxation Station next to Pete's Silly Sideshow and take a break from the day. Bonus points if you take the time to find five of the different Disney character shout-outs on the chairs. (You can also recharge your smart phone battery here while you recharge your own personal battery.)

MK289: Head into Big Top Souvenirs and explore the many shout-outs to the circus. Bonus points if you find the circus rings and trapeze poles.

MK290: Are you feeling a little rumbly in your tumbly? Watch the food artists at Big Top Treats (located in Big Top Souvenirs) make some amazing treats. Bonus points if you try out a specialized caramel apple.

MK291: Meet the circus performers up close and personal. Go to Pete's Silly Sideshow and meet at least two of the four characters: the Great Goofini, the Astounding Donaldo, Minnie Magnifique, or Madame Daisy Fortuna. Bonus points if you meet all four.

MK292: Ride the Walt Disney World Railroad into Storybook Land or out of it. Bonus points if you do both.

MK293: Skip the train and the beaten path, and walk the back path between Storybook Circus and Tomorrowland (you will be just behind Tomorrowland Speedway during your journey). Bonus points if a train passes you or you catch a glimpse of the Contemporary during your stroll.

Dumbo the Flying Elephant

MK294: Before you board, check out both sets of the flying Dumbos (sixteen on each side). Did you notice something different between to the two sets? If you did, take the points.

MK295: Find the artwork panels telling the tale of Dumbo starting with Casey Junior's arrival in town.

MK296: Everyone loves a circus. Find indications that the circus has arrived at the Magic Kingdom. Hint: Be on the lookout for peanut shells, tracks, and footprints.

MK297: Guests have the FastPass+ option, but skip it for this attraction and try the standby line. Get a pager (it will hold your place in line) and try out the play area inside the Big Top. Bonus points if you discover the rope that activates a special lighting effect.

MK298: Up, up, and away. Take flight on Dumbo, but before you board, ask the guests in the Dumbo in front of you if they wouldn't mind taking a picture of you in flight. Bonus points if you are able to return the favor for the guests behind you.

MK299: Take Dumbo to the highest heights. Fly your Dumbo as high as possible. Bonus points if you remain in a state of going up and down.

MK300: If you weren't able to get your picture on the attraction, get a shot of you and your party in a stationary Dumbo outside the attraction. Bonus points if you can mimic being in flight while taking the picture.

The Barnstormer

MK301: In the queue, review the backstory of the Great Goofini's multiple stunts that ended unceremoniously.

MK302: True or False. The Barnstormer roller coaster is over in less than a minute.

MK303: Young guests challenge. Ride Barnstormer as your first roller coaster. Bonus points if you graduate to Big Thunder Mountain in the same trip to the Magic Kingdom.

MK304: During your acrobatic spin in the Great Goofini's plane, find the location that has a very specific outline of where Goofy didn't duck in time.

TOMORROWLAND

MK305: Find the Metrophone and listen to intergalactic banter to find out the latest on what is happening throughout the galaxy.

Tomorrowland Transit Authority (TTA) People Mover

MK306: Discover Walt's vision for the Experimental Prototype Community of Tomorrow (EPCOT) while riding the Tomorrowland Transit Authority PeopleMover.

Fun fact: This exhibit was known as Walt's Progress City and used to be displayed on the second story of Disneyland's Carousel of Progress.

MAGIC KINGDOM

MK307: While riding the TTA, listen for the page for a Mister Tom Morrow. If you hear the page, give yourself some points. Bonus points if you caught the reference to Flight to the Moon and Mr. Johnson.

Fun fact: Flight to the Moon was an attraction in Tomorrowland when the park opened, and both Mr. Johnson and Mr. Morrow were characters from that attraction.

MK308: Did you know that the TTA PeopleMover runs on magnets? Find the magnets along the track as you get pushed and pulled seamlessly throughout your journey.

Fun fact: The use of magnets allows the attraction to run without any emissions.

MK309: If you think Space Mountain might be too much for you to handle, check out the attraction while riding the PeopleMover. Bonus points if you get to go through the Space Mountain section while the lights are on and you can see the track.

MK310: Smile, you are always on camera. Find one of the security cameras watching you during your tour.

MK311: Sit back, relax, and enjoy the view. Guests get a second-story prospective of Tomorrowland as they curve their way around the area. Find all of the following highlights: Tomorrowland Plaza, Tomorrowland Speedway, Buzz Lightyear's Space Ranger Spin, Astro Orbiter, and the path from Tomorrowland to Fantasyland. Bonus points if you spot a parking lot.

MK312: Catch Tomorrowland at night from the sky. Ride the TTA in the evening. Bonus points if you catch the fireworks while you are on the PeopleMover.

MK313: Ride the TTA backwards (always nice to see where you have been).

The Carousel of Progress

MK314: Memorize and sing the attraction's theme song, "There's a Great Big Beautiful Tomorrow," by the time the show ends.

Fun fact: The Sherman Brothers wrote the catchy tune that is performed during each transition.

MK315: Listen carefully to the father's voice and determine what infamous holiday he serves as the narrator for. If you can place it, take the points. Bonus points if you can figure out the famous voice provided for Cousin Orville.

MK316: Watch the three cogs on the attraction sign. What is unique about the information provided?

MK317: In the 1940s scene, find the shout-out to Herb Ryman (attorney-at-law).

Fun fact: Herb Ryman assisted Walt Disney in developing the concept art used to pitch the idea of Disneyland to bankers in New York.

MK318: Find Rover, the dog, in every scene.

Fun fact: In previous versions of the show, the name of the dog changed from scene to scene.

MK319: Locate the following vintage appliances from each era: turn-of-the-last-century, gramophone; 1920s, the radio; 1940s, blender; and the near-present, high-definition televisions.

MK320: Pick out the cultural reference for each era: turn-of-the-last-century, World's Fair in St. Louis; 1920s, Babe Ruth; 1940s, boxing match; and the present: virtual reality games.

MK321: Find a Hidden Mickey. There are four of them in the final scene. Bonus points if you find all four.

Space Mountain

MK322: Step back for a second and examine the structure of the building. Figure out what gives it the out-of-this-galaxy look. If you determined it is because the main structure beams were placed outside the building instead of inside, you've completed the challenge.

MK323: In the queue, play the Space Mountain interactive video game while you prepare for your mission (choose from shooting asteroids, cleaning a runway, or moving cargo).

MK324: Welcome to Starport 75, your intergalactic connection station to anywhere in the galaxy. Ask a cast member what the 75 stands for.

MK326: Countdown to launch, 3, 2, 1, mark...wave goodbye to your countdown launch team as you make your ascent into the "mountain."

MK327: Did you know there are two tracks for Space Mountain (Alpha and Omega)? Complete your space venture on both tracks. Bonus points if you can determine which track is actually longer.

MK328: Complete the ride in the dark and take a guess as to how fast you were going.

MK329: As you blast away while listening to the "Starry-O-Phonic" sound, find the following highlights from your space journey: asteroid, shooting star, comets. Bonus points if you find the final wormhole (pulsating lights all around you) and let out a victory scream.

MK330: You're not alone in space. Count at least three other ride vehicles while you are free falling through space.

Fun fact: The ride vehicles have clear phosphorous lines drawn on them that are illuminated when they pass black lights.

MK331: Once you are done fighting gravity, smile for the ride camera and make it a memorable space venture picture with a terrified pose (hands on face, eyes raised, and mouth open).

Astro Orbiter

MK332: Conquer your fear of heights and board the elevator to the second story to get on your rocket. Enjoy the view of Tomorrowland.

MK333: Ask the guests in the rocket in front of you to capture a picture of you mid-flight. Bonus points if you return the favor for the rocket behind you.

MK334: Take your joystick and raise your rocket all the way to the top for at least two rotations. Bonus points if you weave up and down like you are flying through an asteroid field.

MK335: Want to maximize the feeling that you are flying through space? Ride the Astro Orbiter at night and watch the illuminated planets and galactic space objects zip around you in the dark.

MK336: Name the planets as you zip by them. Give yourself the points if you can name all nine (yes, Pluto still counts as a planet—you're at Disney, after all).

Monsters, Inc. Laugh Floor

MK337: Help produce some "laugh power" by submitting a joke during the pre-show via text (like this one: How do you get a tissue to dance? Put a little boogie in it.) Bonus points if your joke is selected during the show.

MK338: Find Mike Wazowski's dressing room in the queue. Bonus points if you also find the vending machine (be sure you check out the various products).

MK339: True or False. The show uses live actors improvising lines and creating a unique experience each time.

MK340: You don't even have to volunteer. Be part of the show by being selected to either verbally interact with the monsters or have your likeness plastered on the video screen with a humorous caption (hope you don't get the "will treat everyone to churros" caption).

MK341: The ultimate honor for any guest…you are selected to be "that guy." Get chosen by Roz to be "that guy." Be sure you get your "I Was 'That Guy'" sticker after the show.

Buzz Lightyear's Space Ranger Spin

MK342: Get your full briefing from Buzz Lightyear prior to boarding your star cruiser. Bonus points if you get your picture taken with Zurg in the queue.

MK343: Put that laser to the test. Before you start shooting at the Z's, pick a spot to set up your shot parameters (not all the guns shoot straight).

MK344: Drive and shoot at the same time. Hint: Don't be afraid to turn your star cruiser around and shoot at something you may have not seen on the way into a room.

MK345: Find two Hidden Mickeys during your space mission.

MK346: A great space ranger is always aware of his surroundings. Catch sight of the Tomorrowland Transit Authority PeopleMover passing through the attraction as you do battle.

MK347: As you are making the galaxy safe from the Evil Emperor Zurg, find the chickens in the volcano scene.

Fun fact: The chickens are the remains from a previous Delta Dreamflight attraction (one of two previous attractions located here; the other was If You Had Wings.)

MK348: Find a battle buddy and battle it out in your XP-37. If you win, take the challenge points.

Fun fact: The smaller and further the target, the more points they are worth.

MK349: Reach level three (at least 10,001 points) to become a Galactic Hero.

Fun fact: If your vehicle stops, you can keep scoring points.

MK350: Upon exiting the ride and entering the gift shop, find the mural on the wall of different aliens enjoying the sights and sounds of Tomorrowland. Find the rocket ship blasting away that belongs to Stitch.

Stitch's Great Escape!

MK351: Find at least one shout-out to the previous show, ExtraTERRORestrial Alien Encounter (focus on anything with X-S or a character named Skippy).

MK352: Catch the special surprise odor presented during the show. Bonus points if you recognize what that special odor is. More bonus points if you can name one of the other two attractions that highlight a foul odor during the show.

MK353: True or False. The Audio-Animatronic Stitch figure is under three feet tall.

MK354: You've survived Stitch's escape. During the post-escape video, name the Magic Kingdom attraction that Stitch takes flight on after getting kicked out of Cinderella Castle.

MAGIC KINGDOM

MK355: On your way out of the attraction, find the "Days Without an Escape" sign and at least one of the wanted posters (Slushy-523, Poxy-222, Babyfier-151).

Tomorrowland Speedway

MK356: True or False. The cars of Tomorrowland Speedway are faster than the Tomorrowland Transit Authority PeopleMover ride vehicles.

MK357: Find the at least three of the following images in the queue: the Yard of Bricks, Scoring and Timing Pylon, Gasoline Alley, or the Wing and Wheel logo.

MK358: Find at least two of the panels highlighting the various Indianapolis Motor Speedway races: Indy 500, Brickyard 400, or the U.S. Grand Prix at Indianapolis. Bonus points if you find one of the intergalactic race locations (the moon, Saturn, etc).

MK359: Congratulations, you're an adult. Ride with someone else who steers while you push down on the gas pedal (it's bound to happen sometime in your life—it's a rite of passage).

MK360: Cheer on the race car drivers from the observation bridge.

MK361: Master your vehicle. Don't hit the guide track more than twice during your five-minute race. Bonus points if you don't bump the car ahead of you, either.

MK362: Take a picture of yourself while you drive. This is one time where it is okay to take a picture of yourself while behind the wheel.

MK363: Catch the checkered flag when you cross the finish line. Throw your hands in the air to celebrate your victory.

EXTRA MAGIC

MK364: Make use of the PhotoPass photographers (you will find them throughout the park) and try to get a Magic Shot (a little extra magic is added to your photo, like Tinkerbell in your hand). Be sure you ham it up.

MK365: The Magic Kingdom is a popular location for marriage proposals. Be on the lookout for someone on one knee proposing (usually around Cinderella Castle, but you never know). Give yourself double the points if you have met this challenge.

MK366: Experience the Magic Kingdom fireworks on a cruise. Make your reservations early—packages can be as simple as snacks and no music, or a full meal and music that plays with the fireworks.

MK367: This is one of four challenges as a whole. Get a picture with your party at each park icon (Cinderella Castle at Magic Kingdom, Spaceship Earth at Epcot, the Chinese Theatre at Hollywood Studios, and the Tree of Life at Animal Kingdom).

MK368: Go back to your room and take a nap so you can tackle the rest of the day. Bonus points if you stay to closing after taking your nap.

MK369: Pay close attention to when a cast member "points" something out. Ask a cast member directions to an attraction and notice the two-finger point.

Fun fact: Disney uses the two-finger point because it is considered to rude to point with just one finger in some cultures.

MK370: Measure out the number of steps from one trash can to another and try to find one that is more than 30 steps away from another (no cheating with small steps). Bonus points if you notice the different themes of the trash can (based on what land you are in).

MAGIC KINGDOM

Fun fact: When designing the park, Walt Disney examined how long people would carry a piece of trash before dropping it. He came up with 30 steps.

MK371: True or False. You can fit Disneyland into the parking lot area of the Magic Kingdom.

MK372: Catch Tinker Bell flying from the castle, but don't blink, because her flight takes only about 35 seconds. Hint: If you are near The Plaza restaurant, find the wire leading from it to the castle—that will be Tinker Bell's flying route.

Epcot

FUTURE WORLD EAST

EP1: Check out the Art of Disney store. It's almost like being in a Disney-themed museum. Bonus points if you get a little something for home.

EP2: Check out the Leave a Legacy sculptures. Bonus points if you find someone you know.

Fun facts: John Hench designed the plaza. Hench worked for Disney since 1939 and was one of the Imagineers that helped design Disneyland, and served as the art director for Epcot.

EP3: Catch the Fountain of Nations water ballet. Bonus points if you get a shot of the family with the water ballet and Spaceship Earth in the background.

Fun fact: The fountain holds 149,000 gallons of water. Over 24 cultural representatives added a gallon of water from their respective countries to the fountain at its commemoration.

EP4: Be on the lookout for the roaming clean-up crew. Watch the rhythmic flurry of the JAMMitors as they beat out unique performances on trashcans.

Spaceship Earth

EP5: Prior to boarding the attraction, step underneath the sphere and review the pattern of the design.

Fun fact: Spaceship Earth consists of a sphere inside of a sphere, was built in 26 months, and is designed in a way that the triangles help serve as a drainage system when it rains (the water drains into the World Showcase lagoon).

EP6: During the Rome is burning scene, attempt to capture the slight wood-burning scent emitting from the fiery ashes.

EP7: Disney doesn't let a good idea go to waste. Look closely at the faces of the various Audio-Animatronics located throughout the attraction and match at least two up with Audio-Animatronics from other attractions (there are at least 16 matches between Spaceship Earth characters and American Adventure or Hall of Presidents characters).

EP8: True or False. Spaceship Earth weighs at least sixteen million pounds.

EP9: During your journey, find the Egyptian hieroglyphics—they are actual hieroglyphics that a pharaoh used for a royal decree.

EP10: Listen closely to the narrator's voice and determine and try to identify her voice. Bonus points if you can name who we have to thank for the alphabet.

Fun fact: There have been three other narrators: Lawrence Dobkin (*Star Trek*), Walter Cronkite (news anchor), and Jeremy Irons (the voice of Scar from *The Lion King*).

EP11: Listen closely to the music as you move through the attraction. If you noticed the musical styles and instruments were scored for their time period, give yourself the points.

Fun fact: An orchestra of 63 performers and a choir of 24 singers created the musical score.

EP12: Capture Spaceship Earth glowing at night. Bonus points if you catch it on a special night when the magic of projection mapping is being used.

EPCOT

Test Track

EP13: Skip the interactive queue and hit the single-rider line, especially if it's your second visit.

EP14: Skip the single-rider line and design your very own car, built to your specifications. Bonus points if your score is better than everyone else in your ride vehicle. Double bonus points if your car scores over 215.

EP15: Check out the concept vehicles from Chevrolet.

Fun Fact: Test Track replaced World of Motion (sponsored by General Motors) in 1999, and underwent an update in 2012.

EP16: Examine your ride vehicle carefully. Can you find more than four tires/wheels? If so, take the points.

Fun fact: The ride vehicle actually has twenty-two wheels.

EP17: After your test is complete, drop by the photo backdrops on your way out and email yourself a picture of you with your vehicle design.

EP18: True or False. The Test Track layout is more than a mile long.

EP19: After the ride, try a games or simulator in the show room.

EP20: True or False. There are twenty-five cars on the track at one time (including those that are in the loading/unloading area).

Mission: SPACE

EP21: Prepare for takeoff by finding astronauts (past and present) in the queue for Mission: SPACE.

EP22: In the queue, find the picture of the first family to travel in to space (even the dog made the trip). Bonus points if your entire family is making the trip into space also.

EP23: Find the display of the Moon Rover that was used with the Apollo program.

EP24: You've made it to the International Space Training Center. Find the gravity wheel (it's hard to miss because it's 35-feet tall).

Fun fact: The fravity wheel was from the film Mission to Mars.

EP25: Choose wisely—Orange (Mars) or Green (Earth)—your stomach may thank you later. If you can handle the centrifugal force created on the Orange Team mission, go for the full intensity experience. If you want to play it safe, go with the Green Team and explore Earth. Either way, complete a mission and you have completed the challenge. Bonus points if you complete both Orange and Green missions.

EP26: There are four assigned roles (engineer, navigator, commander, pilot). Complete the mission in two of the four roles. Bonus points if you've experienced the attraction in all four roles.

EP27: Find the shout-out to the previous occupant of the Mission: SPACE, Horizons. Look for the gravity wheel with the Horizons logo in the center.

EP28: Try a couple of the interactive games in the Advanced Training Lab. Bonus points if you send a postcard from space to a friend who couldn't go with you.

FUTURE WORLD WEST

EP29: Stop by the Epcot Character Spot and have a meet-and-greet with at least two of the big five (Mickey, Minnie, Donald, Goofy, and Pluto).

EP30: Got a hankering to see what Coca-Cola tastes like around the world? Check out Club Cool in Future

World and serve yourself a few (or a lot) of the Coca-Cola sodas from other countries (Japan, Thailand, South Africa, Africa, Brazil, and Peru). Bonus points if you try the Beverly (Italy) and you like it.

EP31: Have a "bah la la la" moment. Head to Hiro's garage and take a minute to meet Baymax.

The Seas with Nemo & Friends Pavilion

EP32: Upon approaching the Seas with Nemo and Friends Pavilion, find all eight of the characters from the movies and get a snapshot with your favorite. Bonus points if you pause for a second and argue with the seagulls over whose it is—mine!

EP33: Are you SCUBA certified? Try out the ultimate SCUBA adventure at the Seas Pavilion by scuba diving with over 1,200 salt water sea creatures...and who knows, maybe Mickey. Bonus points if you get the backstage tour before or after your dive.

EP34: Not SCUBA certified? Experience the Caribbean Coral Reef with a SCUBA-assisted snorkel on the Seas Aqua Tour.

EP35: No matter your age, participate in the Turtle Talk with Crush show (it's a new adventure each time). Bonus points if you can name the other show at Walt Disney World that uses the real-time animation feature to enable audience participation. Double bonus points if a guest in your group gets to ask Crush (or any of his friends) a question.

EP36: Take the Mr. Ray's pop quiz on the interactive terminals and see how proficient you are with what you have observed in the pavilion. Hint, the answers are all around you.

EP37: Find Mr. Ray's Lagoon and observe the stingrays swimming.

EP38: Head to the Coral Reef restaurant and enjoy a meal as you watch multiple forms of sea life swim by as you dine.

EP39: Get into the belly of the beast, Bruce (the great white shark), and show off your row of teeth. Bonus points if you have more than one person in the photo with you (they need to be inside also).

EP40: Report to Bruce's Sub House and take the time learn a bit more about sharks.

EP41: Find the manatee habitat and watch them eat lettuce. Bonus points if you watch the video about the birth of a baby manatee.

EP42: While viewing the sea life in the large aquarium, find at least three of the five sea creatures: angelfish, dolphin, rays, sea turtle, shark.

Fun fact: There are over six thousand sea creatures in the Sea Base at one time and over sixty different species.

EP43: Enter the world of the nouveau aquariums and find at least three of the five sea creatures in the individual aquariums: clown fish, eel, jellyfish, sea horse, or starfish. Bonus points if you find all five.

EP44: Catch a diver hand-feeding the fish (ask a cast member when it may take place during your visit).

Fun fact: In order for the sharks to not attack the other fish in the aquarium, they are hand fed during the evening hours.

EP45: Check out the dolphin research training or participate in the Dolphins in Depth experience. Bonus points if you catch the visual training methods used by the trainers.

Fun fact: The fish, in general, have also been trained to respond to various signals.

EP46: Find the Hidden Mickey on the bottom of the aquarium floor. Bonus points if you find any other hidden Disney characters that are outlined on the aquarium floor with rocks.

EP47: Find the Life Support Systems Exhibit and don the diver's suit (be sure you get as much of yourself in the suit as possible, including your hands and arms).

EP48: Time for some second-story fun. Increase your aquaculture knowledge by reviewing the farming and husbandry of aquatic animals/plants exhibits. Bonus points if you take advantage of the view from the observation deck while you're up there.

The Seas with Nemo & Friends Attraction

EP49: Help...we lost Nemo again (sort of). Find Nemo at least three times during your expedition.

EP50: Find all of the following characters: Bruce (great white shark), Dory (blue tang), Marlin (clownfish), Mr. Ray (stingray), and Squirt and Crush (turtles).

EP51: Find the Hidden Mickey in the large oyster.

EP52: During your "swim," pick out the animated sea creatures from the live sea creatures.

EP53: Sing-along time. Belt out "Big Blue World" as you complete your undersea voyage.

Fun fact: The song did not come from the movie. The song originated with the Finding Nemo stage show at Disney's Animal Kingdom.

The Land Pavilion

EP54: Check out the fantastic mosaic murals as you enter the Land Pavilion. Bonus points if you noticed that both sides are identical (except that one side has a ruby tile, and the other has an emerald). Double bonus points if you find that one tile on each side.

Fun fact: The murals were built by a father and his daughter (the one different tile represents their birthstone).

EP55: Try a totally unique experience unlike any other experience in a theme park. Take the Behind the Seeds tour and discover the techniques and uncover the secrets of Epcot's science team.

EP56: If you're in the mood for some good old edutainment (that's right, getting educated while you're entertained), watch the Circle of Life: An Environmental Fable video with some of your favorite characters from *The Lion King*. Bonus points if you follow the germination process illustration on the walls.

EP57: Rotate while you meet-and-greet. Have a sit-down meal at the Garden Grill restaurant and meet farmers Chip and Dale (and friends) in all of their farming glory. Bonus points if you catch a glimpse of a Living with the Land boat sailing by as you dine.

Fun fact: Some of the vegetables are actually grown on property in the Living with the Land greenhouse.

Living with the Land

EP58: During your tour, find the number on the mailbox and determine why it was given that number.

EP59: The highlight of the attraction is the various produce, but there are a few critters on the range. Find the animatronic buffalo and prairie dogs.

EPCOT   61

Fun fact: The animatronics for this attraction were originally built for an attraction called Western River Expedition at the Magic Kingdom (the plans were eventually scrapped for Pirates of the Caribbean).

EP60: True or False. The narrator on your cruise is the same one used for the PeopleMover?

Fun fact: The boats used to have cast members riding along and providing narration.

EP61: True or False. The animatronic dog you come across in the farm scene is the same dog from the Carousel of Progress.

Fun fact: The dog was modeled after Walt Disney's dog.

EP62: While reviewing the different plants growing in their biomes, pick out plants that come from at least four different countries.

Fun fact: The Epcot science team can artificially manipulate the heat, lighting, mist, sound, and wind to assist in simulating a perfect environment for plant growth. Bonus points if you notice any of the manipulations used.

EP63: Find a pumpkin in the shape of a Mickey Mouse head.

EP64: True or False. Less than 20 tons of produce is grown in the gardens on an annual basis.

Soarin' Around the World

EP65: Look up, look down, look all around…this time look up and discover the ceiling while you are waiting in the queue. If you noticed that it simulates the effect of clouds in the sky, then take the challenge points. Bonus points if you notice the lighting effect of a cloud passing over you.

EP66: Put your geography skills to the test while you wait to take flight and play the Soarin' Challenge (soarinchallenge.com). Bonus points for unlocking two achievements and two digital passport stamps. Double bonus points if you place on the leaderboard.

EP67: You may recognize your pre-flight host, Patrick Warburton, from the 1990s TV show *Seinfeld*, but name the Disney animated film character that he voices.

EP68: Gone are the orange blossom, pine woods, and sea breeze smell of the Soarin' Over California attraction. But rest easy, they've been replaced with new smells in Soarin's new adventure around the world. See if you can sniff out the scent of roses or fresh grass.

EP69: Upon entrance to the flight deck, examine the mechanical lift (above and behind guests) that is about to take you on an immersive hang gliding trip.

Fun fact: The Imagineer that cracked the code of designing the attraction used an old Erector set to pitch a cantilever system.

EP70: True or False. If you are sitting in the front row, you will be the highest guest in the attraction.

EP71: Welcome to Flight 5505. Figure out the significance of the flight number to complete this challenge. Remember, there's almost always a reason for everything when it comes to Disney attractions.

Fun fact: Soarin' was originally a Disney California Adventure attraction.

EP72: Soarin' debuts with a shot of the Matterhorn and ends with a fireworks display at Walt Disney World, and you will visit 13 unique locations on your journey. Name at least four more by name. Hint: Match them up with the locations that are displayed during the pre-show.

Imagination

EP73: Explore the hands-on playground that is ImageWorks and answer the question on every lab workers mind: "What if?" Finish at least two of the interactive activities to complete the challenge. Bonus points if you email a postcard to a friend.

EP74: Visit the Magic Eye Theater and catch a few Disney and Pixar shorts.

Fun fact: This theater used to house the 3-D show, Captain Eo, starring Michael Jackson.

EP75: Just for fun, and a bit of nostalgia, check out the restrooms in the pavilion. It plays the music from the original attraction.

Journey into Imagination with Figment

EP76: In the queue, find the portraits of the three different Inventor of the Year award winners. Bonus points if you can match the winner with the attraction or movie.

EP77: True or False. Figment was one of the first characters to be created solely for use as part of an attraction.

EP78: Figment pops up throughout the adventure. Locate him at least five times.

Fun fact: The Imagineers decided to make Figment purple instead of green because the sponsor's (Kodak Film) main rival (Fuji Film) used green as its main color.

EP79: There are at least three Hidden Mickeys located throughout the attraction. Find at least one to complete the challenge. Hint: Check out the dry-erase board or the headphones in the sight room, and focus on the word "action" in the final room. Bonus points if you find all three Hidden Mickeys.

EP80: Join in on the Sherman Brothers' rendition of "One Little Spark" at any time during your journey.

EP81: Find the shout-out to the original host of the show, Dreamfinder.

WORLD SHOWCASE

EP82: Find an inexpensive personalized gift. For example, you can get a genuine leather bracelet or key chain with free engraving at Epcot's Canada Pavilion or at the Magic Kingdom in Frontierland or the Pirates of the Caribbean gift shop. Bonus points if you get ring engraved with your initials in the Mexico Pavilion.

EP83: Get a picture with one cast member from each of the eleven countries represented (the costumes are specific to the country). Bonus points if you ask at least three cast members about their costumes. Double bonus points if you get a group picture with the Voices of Liberty ensemble.

EP84: Experience Epcot's IllumiNations fireworks on a cruise. Make your reservations early—packages can be as simple as snacks and no music, to a full meal and music that plays with the fireworks.

EP85: Ask at least two different cast members (from different countries) about their homeland.

EP86: Most of the Disney theme parks only have one guest entrance; Epcot has two. Take the path less traveled and enter or exit the park through the entrance located between France and the United Kingdom pavilions. Bonus points if you spend some leisurely time around the Boardwalk area.

EPCOT

EP87: Find the classic Mickey in the clock at the World Showcase park entrance.

EP88: Agent 007 has nothing on Disney's favorite platypus, Perry. Take the Agent P World Showcase Adventure challenge and uncover the clues in the Mexico, China, Germany, Italy, Japan, France, and United Kingdom pavilions to help Major Monogram and the Agency bring down Dr. Doofenshmirtz.

EP89: Check in at the Kidcot Fun Stop in at least six of the eleven World Showcase pavilions. Bonus points if you complete the Kidcot Fun Stop in each pavilion.

Mexico Pavilion

EP90: Stop and explore the Mexico Folk Art Gallery featuring Oaxacan wood carvings. Bonus points if you discover the Spanish words for each of the eight categories—from Los Cominenzos (the beginning) to El Dia de los Muertos (the Day of the Dead).

EP91: Catch the energetic Mariachi Cobre ensemble and sing along with the performers.

EP92: Hola, Senor Donald. Catch Donald Duck sporting a serape and sombrero for a meet-and-greet. Bonus points if you greet him with your best Donald Duck impersonation.

EP93: Sit back at the San Angel Inn and enjoy a meal (or tasty Mexican dessert) while you watch the boats of the Gran Fiesta Tour float by a volcano.

EP94: Find the fountain in the Mexico Pavilion, make your wish, and toss in a coin. Bonus points if you wished for another Disney vacation in the next year.

EP95: Watch a cast member craft a glass figurine. Bonus points if you take home a glass souvenir.

EP96: Get your sweet tooth fix while watching the fireworks. Enjoy some churritos with caramel sauce as you take in IllumiNations.

EP97: On the Gran Fiesta Tour, help Panchito and Jose find Donald. Locate that crazy duck at least three times during your cruise.

EP98: Name the other Walt Disney World attraction that uses the same child-like animatronics.

EP99: Wave to the diners enjoying a meal at the San Angel Inn as you pass by the Mayan pyramid.

Fun fact: The idea of an attraction next to a restaurant originated with the Pirates of the Caribbean attraction and the Blue Bayou restaurant in Disneyland.

EP100: During your Gran Fiesta tour of Mexico, discover three different Mexican cities.

Norway Pavilion

EP101: Pick out two of the four distinct architectural styles (Setesdal, Bergen, Oslo, and Alesund). Bonus points if you find the buildings with grass on the rooftops (animals will often maintain the grass in Norway, but not at Epcot).

EP102: Find the waterfall and capture a fantastic photo op.

EP103: Find the large troll statue in the Puffin's Roost shop and get your family Christmas card picture knocked out with the troll. Bonus points if you find at least two trolls in the gardens.

EP104: Venture into the Stave Church and check out various Norwegian displays (how Norway influenced *Frozen*). Bonus points if you find the Viking rune stone sporting Norse dialect.

EPCOT

EP105: Head to the Royal Sommerhaus cabin and seek out a meet-and-greet with the royal sisters from Arendelle, Anna and Elsa. Bonus points if you can recite "Let It Go" from memory while you wait in line.

EP106: They may look like costumes to guests, but engage with a cast member to find out about their traditional attire, the bunad (red vest, white shirt, and dark skirt or pants).

EP107: When in Norway, eat like a Norwegian, or at least snack like one. Try a traditional lefse (cinnamon, sugar, and butter on rolled potato bread).

EP108: Enjoy a parade of princesses while you eat. Report to Akershus Royal Banquet Hall and relish a Norwegian buffet with princesses. Bonus points if any member of your party joins in on the parade.

EP109: Find the window opening filled with bricks (focus on the second story).

Fun fact: At one time, Norwegians were taxed based on how many windows they had in their home. In order to evade the tax, they would place bricks in the window opening.

EP110: Explore the Mmedieval décor in Akershus (designed after the actual Akershus in Oslo).

EP111: Strike a pose with the Viking statue outside the Stave Church.

Fun fact: The statue is that of King Olaf II, the patron saint of Norway.

EP112: On Frozen Ever After, find the royal proclamation declaring a Summer Snow Day Celebration.

EP113: True or False. The voice actors that you hear throughout the attraction are the same voice actors from the movie *Frozen*.

EP114: Find three trinkets in Oaken's Trading Post and the sign "Official Ice Master & Deliverer of Arendelle."

EP115: While you're on the ride, find the snow babies from *Frozen Forever* (the follow-up Disney short) and the dresses worn by Anna and Elsa.

EP116: It wouldn't be *Frozen* without a chance for a sing along. Warm up those pipes and sing "Let It Go" with Queen Elsa before you plunge backwards.

China Pavilion

EP117: Take in some amazing and breath-taking feats of agility, balance, and strength with the Jeweled Dragon Acrobats. Bonus points if you can pull off any of their impressive acts.

EP118: Stand in the middle of the Temple of Heaven and listen for your voice to reverberate back to the spot you are located.

EP119: While you're there, center yourself in the room and look straight up at the dome. Notice the perfect 360-degree symmetry. Bonus points if you can figure out the two meanings of the twelve columns supporting the outside and the four columns closer to the center.

EP120: Find the Terracotta Army (replicas of the original that were discovered in 1974 and dated back to 210 BC). Bonus points if you notice five detailed differences between different army figures.

EP121: Beat the heat with a personalized fan. Pick out a fan and have a cast member personalize it with your name written in Chinese.

EP122: Roam around the serene garden and find at least one form of wildlife, like frogs.

EP123: Attend the Reflections of China Circle-Vision movie and find the following highlights during the film: the Great Wall of China, Hunan, Shanghai, the Forbidden City, and Hong Kong. Bonus points if you explore the display room while waiting for the film.

EP125: Check out the Nine Dragons restaurant, and try your hand at calligraphy by drawing out Chinese characters on a placemat.

EP126: Return in the evening to see the China Pavilion lit up in all its glory.

EP127: Ni hao. Say hello to Mulan (and maybe Mushu) during a character meet-and-greet. Bonus points if you hear "Reflections" being sung while you meet her.

EP128: Travel back in time musically and catch Si Xian as the cast members play the Chinese zheng (a harp-like instrument).

The Outpost

EP129: Find the three canoes and take a picture of your party getting ready to ply the waterways to catch some fish.

EP130: Find the burlap bag containing the kola nuts. Bonus points if you find the Chevy Woody (sporting Coke products).

Fun fact: Kola nuts come from a tree native to Western Africa. They provide caffeine and flavoring to Coca-Cola products.

EP131: Burn some energy (if you have any left) on the djembe (tapered drum). Bonus points if you can play a tune that other guests can recognize.

EP132: Stop by Mnundo Kibanda and watch a cast member carve out a piece of art.

EP133: Hunters' camouflage, fearsome warrior, or spiritual expression can be captured with paint. Try a face painting to display your cultural relevance.

EP134: Take a few minutes and watch the magic unfold. Go to the drawbridge between the Outpost and China and watch the launching of Illumination islands at 5pm.

Germany Pavilion

EP135: Gutentag ("hello" in German). Seek out the fountain featuring St. George slaying the dragon and strike your best dragon slaying pose for the camera.

EP136: March into the Karamell-Kuche and latch on to the smell of fresh caramel being made right in front of you. Bonus points if you get some caramel to help you tackle the rest of the World Showcase.

EP137: If you are in the Germany courtyard at the top of the hour, find the clock and watch the German boy and girl appear from the clock and twirl.

EP138: Walt Disney loved trains and Mickey Mouse. Find the Hidden Mickey at the miniature train and village on the outskirts of the Germany Pavilion. Hint: Focus on church near the lagoon.

Fun fact: The model railroad and garden village were built for the Flower and Garden Festival; however, it proved so popular that Disney decided to maintain it year around.

EP139: Find the large mural on the back wall of the pavilion and give it a knock. Now guess as to why there is a hollow sound. If you're stumped, ask a cast member (or go to the back of the book to get the answer).

EP140: Channel your inner Oktoberfest and sing along with German folk singers at the Biergarten buffet.

EPCOT

Bonus points if you finish off a schnitzel, a pretzel, and a beer all in one sitting. Double bonus points if you get up and do the Chicken Dance (wait until they play the song, though).

EP141: Find the Black Forest cuckoo clocks and some impressive beer steins while you're at it. Bonus points if you ring a cow bell.

EP142: It's Christmas every day at die Weihnachts Ecke. Check out the Christmas decorations and learn the story of the Christmas Pickle. Bonus points if you buy one and place it in your Christmas tree.

Italy Pavilion

EP143: Try one of the three restaurants here (Tutto Italia Ristorante, Via Napoli, or Tutto Gusto Wine Cellar). Bonus points if you get a wood-fired pizza pie.

Fun fact: The three wood-burning ovens represent three active volcanoes in Italy (Stromboli, Etna, and Vesuvio).

EP144: Get a snap shot on the bridge near the lagoon. Choose between the lagoon and Spaceship Earth as your backdrop or the Italy Pavilion (or go crazy and get both). Double bonus points if you catch someone proposing at this location. Triple bonus points if you are the one proposing or being proposed to!

EP145: Indulge your sweet tooth. Have some mouth-watering Italian ice cream (gelato). Bonus points if you get a gelato sandwich.

EP146: Catch Sergio the mime in all his glory. Bonus points if you get selected to participate in the act.

EP147: Find the pillars decorated with kings, locate the king with the bowling balls, and then find the Hidden Mickey on the bowling ball.

EP148: Find the red button (located behind the stores) with the sign that requests that you "press for a surprise." Press that button. Bonus points if you got someone wet when you pressed the button.

EP149: Buon giorno, Neptune! Find the Fontana de Nettuno and get a group picture with Neptune.

Fun fact: The fountain was inspired by the famous Italian sculptor Bernini.

EP150: Find the angel with authentic gold leaf overlooking the pavilion. Hint: Look up, way up.

EP151: The pavilion is rich with historical Italian architecture re-created just for Epcot. Find the following: Doge's Palace, Saint Mark's Campinile (the bell tower), and the columns of San Marco and San Todaro.

The American Adventure Pavilion

EP152: Find the clock as you enter the pavilion from the Italy side and find the abnormal Roman numeral. Bonus point if you can site another location at the Magic Kingdom that follows suit.

EP153: Examine the American Adventure building and see if you can tell how Imagineers made a five-story building like a two-and-a-half-story building.

Fun fact: Imagineers had to use forced perspective because a five-story building during colonial times did not exist, and a two-and-a-half-story building would have been too miniscule from across the World Showcase Lagoon for guests to see.

EP154: Catch the Voices of Liberty in all of their a cappella glory in the rotunda prior to the American Adventure show. Bonus points if you see the Voices of Liberty perform during the Candlelight Processional.

EP155: Review at least six of the eleven paintings on your way up to see the American Adventure show.

EP156: Once inside the theatre, take a moment and review at least six of the twelve "Spirits of America" statues. Bonus points if you review all twelve (half before the show, half after).

EP157: Review the Hall of Flags exhibit and examine the multitude of flags that have represented the United States. Bonus points if you find the America flag that flew over the wreckage of 9/11/2001.

EP158: Catch a performance of the Spirit of America Fife and Drum Corps.

EP159: Attend an event in the "secret lounge" in the upstairs portion of the American Adventure building.

EP160: Watch a show or concert at the America Gardens Theater. Bonus points if it is the Candlelight Processional.

Japan Pavilion

EP161: Watch a cast member in the Mitsukoshi Department Store crack open an oyster to recover its pearl. Bonus points if you purchase a pearl to remember your trip to Walt Disney World.

Fun Fact: The cast members used to dive into the water to recover the oysters for guests that wanted to buy a pearl.

EP162: It's like listening to thunder after the lightning. Catch the rhythmic beating of the drums with choreographed dancing of the Matsuriza ensemble playing traditional Japanese Taiko drums.

Fun fact: The Taiko drummers perform on the five-story pagoda (Goju-no-to). Each story represents a different element in the universe: earth, fire, sky, water, and wind.

EP163: Explore the garden and find the Japanese maples, monkey puzzle trees, bamboo, and banzai trees.

Fun fact: Gardening in Japan is considered a precise art and is labor intensive.

EP164: Capture a shot with the Torii gate and Spaceship Earth in the background.

EP165: Take a break from the hustle and bustle. Find the koi fish swimming in the pond in the garden.

Fun fact: Japanese Koi are symbols of love and friendship.

EP166: Be entertained while you eat. Dine at Teppan Edo and watch the master chef chop and fry your meal right in front of you.

EP167: Find the two samurai warriors on horses while crossing the bridge leading to the castle.

EP168: Enter White Heron Castle and explore the Bijutsu-kan Gallery. Bonus points if it is an exhibit that you are familiar with (exhibits rotate).

EP169: Find the lantern statue (toward the exit to Morocco). There are no distinct markings.

Fun fact: The statue was a gift from the emperor of Japan to Roy E. Disney at the opening of the Magic Kingdom. It was moved to the Japan Pavilion when Epcot opened.

EP170: Hello Kitty, Tamagotichis (Japanese footwear), and anime are only the beginning. Discover the extensive selection of Japanese souvenirs in the Mitsukoshi Department Store. Bonus points if you sample a bit of sake in the back of the store.

Fun fact: The original Mitsukoshi Department Store is considered the oldest department store in the world, dating back at least three hundred years.

Morocco Pavilion

EP171: Dive into the culture and lifestyle of Morocco. Visit the Gallery of Arts and History and the Fez house (representative of a Moroccan home).

Fun fact: Listen carefully for the sound of children playing as you get near the fountain.

EP172: Take a close look from faraway. From the World Showcase Lagoon (preferably on a boat), look directly at the Morocco Pavilion and find the Twilight Zone Tower of Terror.

Fun fact: In order to preserve the magic, Imagineers had to ensure that the tower's color scheme and style were designed to ensure that it blended with the architecture of the buildings in Morocco.

EP173: Dine at Restaurant Marrakesh, enjoy some couscous and lamb, and be bedazzled by the belly dancer. Bonus points if you are selected to try your hand at belly dancing.

EP174: Celebrate like Iron Man and the Avengers. Check out Tangerine Café and try some shawarma. Bonus points if you get some baklava to top it off.

EP175: Find the Bab Boujouloud Gate (fashioned after the gateway to Fez) and take notice of how the gate serves as a separation point from the old city of Medina.

EP176: Examine the detailed tile work and mosaics located throughout the pavilion.

Fun fact: King Hassan II provided Moroccan artists to work with Disney Imagineers to create various mosaics throughout the pavilion. Note that there are no depictions of humans or animals in any of the art work due to their religious significance.

EP177: Find the Hidden Mickey featuring three brass plates. Hint: They are on a door.

EP178: Get lost in the bazaar in the back of the pavilion. Guests will feel like they aren't in Epcot.

EP179: Find the camel sporting the red fez and snap a picture with it. Bonus points if you put a fez on your head for the picture.

EP180: During IllumiNations, take a look at the Morocco Pavilion and figure out what is different about it compared to the pavilions around it.

EP181: Take advantage of the unique meet-and-greet location for Jasmine, Aladdin, and Genie.

France Pavilion

EP182: Look for a part of the pavement on your way in to France from Morocco that stands out from the rest of the pavement (this represents the Straits of Gibraltar).

EP183: Get a caricature done of someone in your party at the French Pavilion. Bonus points if two or more in your party are in the same caricature.

EP184: Hold on to your Mickey Ears and watch Serveur Amusant featuring French acrobats who captivate the crowd with their astonishing balance and coordination.

EP185: Sit back and relax while watching Impressions de France. Your challenge is to recognize at least five distinct French locations (Cannes, Seine, Alps, etc).

Fun fact: The theater utilizes a 200-degree wide-screen view and the music was produced in London by the National Philharmonic.

EPCOT

EP186: The France Pavilion is tres magnifique for character (Aurora from *Sleeping Beauty* and Marie from *Aristocats*) meet-and-greets. Score a shot with at least one Disney character while in France. Bonus points if you get a picture with both.

EP187: Make Ratatouille proud and have a meal at either Chefs de France or Monsieur Paul. If you want to keep it light, try a pastry at Les Halles Boulangerie & Paitisserie to complete the challenge.

EP188: The France Pavilion highlights an urban ambiance at its finest. Explore the positioning of the trees and how they are pruned to discover how Imagineers produced the illusion of distance.

EP189: Wine connoisseur? Drop in and take a lesson on the wines of France at the Vins de France. Bonus points if you try the wine passport and sample a bit in France, Germany, and Italy.

EP190: Follow the cobblestone streets to the fountain. Take a few minutes to sit at the fountain and people watch while you enjoy listening to the romantic background music.

EP191: True or False. The Eiffel Tower replica was built using the same blueprints as the original built in Paris by Gustave Eiffel.

Fun fact: Epcot's Eiffel Tower was built at one-tenth scale to the original. The top of the tower has special paint on it to dishearten birds from nesting there.

EP192: As you cross the footbridge from the United Kingdom to France, find at least two of the items left behind by French residents.

Fun fact: The footbridge was inspired by the Pont des Arts Bridge in France.

EP193: Take note as you cross the bridge from France to the United Kingdom. What famous waterway is represented under the bridge?

United Kingdom Pavilion

EP194: Find the red phone booths and see how many people can fit in one of them for a unique photo op.

EP195: Take a closer look at the chimneys. If you noticed the hand-painted smoke stains, take the points.

EP196: No trip to the United Kingdom is complete without a visit to the Hat Lady. Enjoy the musical tunes and lively pianist renderings of the Hat Lady at the Rose and Crown Dining Room and Pub (and even learn the stories behind a few of the hats).

EP197: Tackle the waist-high (to an adult) hedge maze at the back of the pavilion. Bonus points if you complete it without getting blocked.

EP198: Head into the Historical Research Center and find your family's coat of arms. Bonus points if your coats of arms is already on display.

EP199: From the outside of the Rose and Crown, examine the façade and find the three different styles that were used by Imagineers when they designed it (country pub, street pub, and waterfront pub).

Fun fact: The name Rose and Crown was selected because these two words were the most popular words used in naming pubs across the United Kingdom.

EP200: Pay attention to the architecture. Discover its progression from the 1600s thatched roofs, to the 1700s higher ceilings, and then the 1800s neoclassical design with stone. Bonus points if you spot the chimney reminiscent of a scene from *Mary Poppins*.

EP201: The United Kingdom is bursting with character meet-and-greets (Winnie the Pooh, Tigger, Eeyore, Mary Poppins, Alice in Wonderland). Meet at least two of the characters while you are there.

EP202: Explore the Butterfly and Knot herb garden. Pay close attention to the chrysalis box for cocoons (notice that there is no bottom so that the butterflies can fly away when they break through their cocoon). Bonus points if you see a butterfly.

EP203: Catch a latest British invasion band playing in the pavilion. Bonus points if you score some fish and chips to eat while you are enjoying the show.

EP204: Find the crest for the four of the higher education institutions in the United Kingdom (Cambridge, Edinburgh, Eton, and Oxford). Hint: Look in the windows at the Queen's Table.

Canada Pavilion

EP205: Find the three totem poles and determine what the story each is relaying.

Fun fact: The totem poles were carved by Tsimshian artisan David Boxley. The Raven totem pole was put on display in at Epcot in 1998 and the other two (Eagle and Whale) in 2017.

EP206: Find forced perspective at its finest—a three-story building that uses five levels of windows to make it appear larger.

EP207: Take in the sights and sounds of the waterfall. Wear your rain gear if you need to.

Fun fact: The waterfall actually masks the sounds of a nearby generator.

EP208: Time to spoil yourself. Have dinner at Le Cellier Steakhouse.

EP209: Examine the plants in the Rocky Mountain area. If you notice that the plants at the bottom are much larger than the plants on top, then you have uncovered an Imagineer's forced perspective magic.

EP210: A Canadian garden in Florida? Discover Victoria Gardens and find the following: maple trees (honors Canada's national symbol), white flowers (to mimic the snow), and the house that looks like it is hidden in the hillside. Bonus points if you catch sight of a duck or a rabbit in the gardens.

Fun fact: The garden was inspired by Butchart Gardens in British Columbia.

EP211: Find the railings with cutouts of maple leaves in them.

EP212: Head to the Maple Leaf Mine and catch "O' Canada!" in all of its 360-degree Circle-Vision glory and catch at least four different areas of Canada (Niagara Falls is a given).

EP213: Catch an ode to some of Canada's best songwriters and watch the group Alberta Bound bring the Mill Stage to life.

Fun fact: Alberta Bound is a song by Gordon Lightfoot, one of Canada's most famous entertainers.

EP214: Report to the Rocky Mountain Kodak picture area before IllumiNations begins and see the opening of the rock formation to uncover lighting and sound equipment for the evening's entertainment. Bonus points if you get a picture of it.

Hollywood Studios

HOLLYWOOD BOULEVARD

HS1: Relive the Golden Age of Hollywood. Chat with a Citizen of Hollywood. Choose between the starlet, gossip columnist, talent agent, aspiring actor, faded star, director, or even the police officer. Bonus points if the director wants to cast you in the next production.

HS2: Get the feel of the times. Check in at Sid Cahuenga's One-of-a-Kind bungalow and catch some 1930s phonograph music. Bonus points if you go in to take care of some MyMagic+ business while you're at it.

HS3: Vroom, vroom, vroom was a common sound in southern California. Get cultured in car memorabilia at Oscar's Classic Car souvenirs.

HS4: Get a feel for a turn of the-last-century railway station. Examine the Trolley Car Café as you load up on a special treat or some Starbucks (or just check it to see what original public transportation looked like in Los Angeles).

HS5: Seek out a little "California Crazy." Find the Art Deco architecture featuring a larger-than-life camera and get a picture with it.

HS6: Time for the guest to be a star. Head to Cover Story and get your mugshot (ah, headshot) plastered on the magazine of your choice.

HS7: Explore Mickey's of Hollywood and find the shout-outs to early Mickey. Find all three of the

Mickey statues: Steamboat Willie Mickey, Band Concert Mickey, and Sorcerer's Apprentice Mickey.

HS8: Check out the dentist directory for the second floor of Keystone Clothiers, and marvel in hysterical dentist names.

HS9: Park yourself in front of the Chinese Theater and prepare to be taken to a galaxy far, far away. Catch the Star Wars extravaganza with lasers, movie projection on the theater façade, and fireworks. Bonus points if you take in the show while enjoying the Star Wars Galactic Spectacular Dessert Party.

HS10: When in Rome (or Hollywood) do as the Romans. Head to the Hollywood Brown Derby restaurant and relive a southern California classic dining experience in an authentic replica of the original. Bonus points if you try the famous Cobb salad or grapefruit cake.

HS11: Explore the walls of the Hollywood Brown Derby that are decorated with caricatures of some of Hollywood's biggest stars of years past.

Fun fact: The caricatures in the black frames are copies of the originals, and the ones in the gold frames are the originals from the Brown Derby in Hollywood.

HS12: Try a truly unique experience and dine with a Disney Imagineer in the Bamboo Room at the Hollywood Brown Derby.

ECHO LAKE

HS13: Repeat after me: I am one with the force, the force is with me. Report to the Sound Studio and catch the ten-minute tribute to Star Wars: Path of the Jedi.

HS14: Get some of Mom's home cooking at the 50's Prime Time Café. Travel back to the 1950s, catch some

HOLLYWOOD STUDIOS

Mickey Mouse Club on the black-and-white television, and get served by "Mom" to complete the challenge. Bonus points if you are told to "keep your elbows off the table."

HS15: Get a picture with Gertie the Dinosaur (you can't miss her). Bonus points if you get a picture while enjoying some ice cream from Dinosaur Gertie's Ice Cream of Extinction.

Fun fact: In 1914, Gertie the Dinosaur became the first animated film as part of Winsor McCay's vaudeville act.

HS16: Experience the 1950s in the Tune-In Lounge and watch a little *Leave It to Beaver* why you are at it.

HS17: If you have young'uns that love Playhouse Disney characters, head to Hollywood & Vine and enjoy a buffet during your character meet-and-greet. Bonus points if anyone in your party joins in during the "random" dance routines.

HS18: Study the nautical flags (letters) and pennants (numbers) between smokestacks at Min & Bill's Dockside Diner. Figure out what the letters spell out.

HS19: In front of Min and Bill's Diner, find at least two of the wooden prop crates and check out the recipient and addresses (a homage to classic characters and movies).

HS20: Drop in on Olaf at the Celebrity Spotlight and see if you can melt the lovable and carefree snowman during your photo op.

For the First Time in Forever

HS21: Recapture the magic of *Frozen* by signing along with the royal historians of Arendelle. Bonus points if you don't need the subtitles to remember the lyrics.

HS22: Capture a bit of the indoor snowfall in your hands (but be sure to "let it go" before it melts).

Indiana Jones Stunt Spectacular

HS23: Be on the lookout for a rope dangling outside of the Indiana Jones Stunt Show with a very directive sign. Pay no attention to the sign and pull on the rope. Then listen to the sounds of the workers below.

HS24: Volunteer to be an "extra" on the set (don't worry, you won't have to perform any stunts). If you're really motivated, show lots of enthusiasm and sit toward the front of the theater. Bonus points if you get selected to participate in the show.

HS25: True or False. The giant (twelve feet in diameter) rolling boulder weighs over a ton.

HS26: Hang out after the show and get your picture with Indiana Jones or Marian. Bonus points if you are wearing an Indiana Jones hat in the picture.

Star Tours

HS27: While waiting for your Star Tours flight to begin, check out as many of the different luggage scans as you can (there are 71 in all—check out at least five for the points). The scans range from an Ewok playing the drums on some poor stormtrooper's armor to Buzz Lightyear.

HS28: Listen for Egroeg Sacul to be paged. Bonus points if you heard it and figured out it was George Lucas, the creator of the Star Wars universe, pronounced backwards.

HS29: Pay close attention to the pre-board video and find the stuffed Mickey Mouse. Hint: Focus on the Ewoks entering the Starspeeder.

HS30: Star Tours offers 54 different experiences (locations such as the Death Star, and characters like Darth Vader). Your challenge is to visit at least three different planets and come across three different characters. However, you do not control your fate—the attraction selects these experiences for you randomly.

HS31: Pick out the Rebel spy on your flight. Bonus points if you just happen to be that Rebel spy.

HS32: During your flight, pick out the famous line on the attraction that's been in all the Star Wars movies. Hint: Han Solo was the first one to utter it.

HS33: Hop on the Imperial Speeder outside the attraction and capture a picture of someone in your party escaping a stormtrooper. Bonus points if you get a picture of someone doing battle with the AT-AT.

HS34: Build your own light saber or droid at Tatooine Traders, or try out a Jedi robe. Bonus points if you buy the shirt with Darth Vader riding the carrousel.

HS35: Stroll by the Ewok Village at night and check out the moon of Endor. Bonus points if you saw the camp fire and heard Ewoks talking.

Jedi Training Academy

HS36: Do you have a young Padawan in your group? Report to the Jedi Training Academy (do it early) to sign up your child for admittance to the stage for Jedi training. You can also earn the points if you watch the show and cheer on the Padawans as they face off against the Dark Side.

HS37: Cheer on the Padawans when they face Darth Vader. Bonus points if you boo when Darth Vader makes his grand appearance.

HS38: Get in the spirit of the moment. Hum any one of the theme songs that they play during the show (no heavy breathing Vader style, though).

GRAND AVENUE

HS39: Find the Hidden Mickey lookalike in the Miss Piggy Fountain in the courtyard. Hint: It might look a bit like Waldo from the show.

HS40: Explore the walls throughout the courtyard. Find the shout-out to the Swedish Chef and Rizzo Rat.

HS41: Explore the gift shop and find the wanted poster in German for Kermit the Frog. Bonus points if you also find the Chickens Only sign.

HS42: The eyes have it. Find at least two sets of eyes (one has wings) in plain sight (focus on a lamp overhead, and above Miss Piggy's clock).

HS43: Even though the Grand Avenue (formerly Muppet's Courtyard) is somewhat new, there are still upgrades taking place. Find at least two new paint jobs splattered throughout the courtyard.

HS44: Aerosmith isn't the only rock band rocking at Hollywood Studios. Find the Electric Mayhem band in the Muppet Gift Shop. Bonus points if you do your best Animal impersonation once you find them.

HS45: Look up, way up, in the Muppet gift shop. Find the hallway of dressing rooms that is a shout-out to *The Muppet Show* from the 1970s.

HS46: See the fun Muppet caricatures in PizzeRizzo.

Fun fact: PizzeRizzo is fashioned after a New York-style pizza restaurant and named after a rat.

HS47: Explore Mama Melrose's Ristorante Italiano and find the Legends of Disney's Hollywood Studios display. Bonus points if you stop in for a meal.

Muppet Vision 3D

HS48: Review the directory (and "the rest of the directory") prior to entering the Muppets Vision 3D World Headquarters. Bonus points for considering to pay extra for "no soup." (Find the soup of the day reference—you'll get it.)

HS49: Wander around the pre-show area and find at least one of the visual puns (think Annette Funicello which rhymes with Jell-O).

HS50: Get to the Muppet*Vision 3-D show in time to experience the pre-show movie (yes, you can sit on the floor and relax while you watch it). Bonus points if you can quote some of it.

HS51: While waiting for the show, find the sign hanging over the door to the security office. Read the sign and lift the mat. Note the irony.

HS52: Explore the queue area to check out the multitude of movie posters using various Muppet characters spoofing films of yesteryear.

HS53: Pay close attention to Statler and Waldorf at the end of the show and determine what is special about their arms when they wave their white flags. If you answered, "the arms aren't attached to the animatronics, but connected separately to the symphony box... thus giving each three arms," take the points.

HS54: Sight isn't the only sense tickled in 3-D. Enter the fourth dimension and experience all three of the following during the show: gust of air, water being squirted at you, and soap bubbles.

PIXAR PLACE

HS55: Leave no man behind! Catch an Army Man and get a picture for posterity.

HS56: This place is more fun than a barrel of monkeys. Speaking of which, find the multi-colored monkeys that escaped the barrel. Hint: Look up.

HS57: Head on over to Woody's Picture Shootin' Corral and get a picture with the rootinest, tootinest cowboy in the west (Woody)—and his pal Buzz Lightyear while you're at it. Bonus points if you score another member of the Toy Story gang.

HS58: Find the upside-down oversized version of Battleship (the game).

Toy Story Midway Mania

HS59: Count the number of different games that you find throughout the queue. If you find more than five, you've completed the challenge. Bonus points for counting how many of these same games that you've played before. If it is five or more, take the bonus points.

HS60: Catch the hilarious Mr. Potato Head animatronic. Bonus points if you sing or tell a joke with him.

Fun fact: Insult comic Don Rickles voiced Mr. Potato Head in the movies and for the animatronic.

HS61: True or False. While guests are traveling through the queue in Andy's bedroom, guests are made to feel about the size of a toy.

HS62: You will play five Toy Story-themed carnival midway mini-games. Beat your ride mate in at least three of the five mini-games to earn the points. Bonus points if you dominate your opponent during Woody's Roundup shooting gallery (the finale).

HS63: At the end of the queue, get a picture of you and those in your party sporting your 3-D glasses.

HS64: Get to firing your cannon (pulling your pull string) and uncover some special effects (blast of air or spritz of water). Bonus points if you get shot with both air and water.

HS65: There's gold in them there hills…or at least some extra magic incorporated during your tour through Toy Story Mania. Uncover at least two of the hidden "Easter eggs" with a blast of your cannon to reveal a game change or extra targets.

ANIMATION COURTYARD

HS66: Visit the Animation Gallery and view Disney fine art, animation cels, and collectibles. Bonus points if you take a little piece of the magic home with you.

Disney Junior—Live on Stage

HS67: The action is fast and furious throughout the show, so don't blink for long. Sing along with at least two of the songs.

Fun fact: There are twenty-five different characters that perform twenty-five songs.

HS68: Take a look up and all around inside Mickey's Clubhouse. Find the multiple lighting fixtures that help bring the show to life.

Fun fact: There are approximately 400 light fixtures used during the show.

HS69: True or False. All of the character voices in the show are performed by the same voice actors that voice the characters on their Disney Channel show.

HS70: Don't let the kids have all the fun. If you have little ones, get up and join them in some movement. Bonus points if you catch some of the falling confetti.

Star Wars Launch Bay

HS71: Get your Star Wars geek on and try out a special character encounter. Select either the dark side with Kylo Ren or the light side with Chewbacca, and get your picture taken with Star Wars royalty. Hint: Do not wear a Boba Fett or Darth Vader shirt in to see Chewbacca. He may put you in the corner. Bonus points if you meet both of these characters.

HS72: Channel your inner scum and villainy and visit the cantina area. Find the holo-chess game there.

HS73: Watch the video in Launch Bay Theater for inside information from directors, writers, and producers.

HS74: Immerse yourself in the galaxy of Star Wars and check out at least two of the three galleries: Celebration Gallery, Celebration Hallway, or Preview Gallery. Bonus points if you check out all three.

HS75: This is the droid you are looking for. Drop in and meet BB-8 and get a picture.

Voyage of the Little Mermaid

HS76: As you prepare to go undersea, find at least two of these items: fishing net, a shark, a diver's suit. Bonus points if you find King Triton's trident.

HS77: Pay close attention to the lasers when the show begins and find the Hidden Mickey.

HS78: Feel like you are beside the ocean and sit close enough to the stage to feel the ocean breeze and sea mist to complete the challenge.

HOLLYWOOD STUDIOS

HS79: True or False. Sebastian and his hot crustacean band is joined onstage by over a hundred different puppets as he croons about life "under the sea."

HS80: You can't stop your toes from tapping and you can't keep a song from being sung after this show. Sing (or hum) one of the songs as you depart the theater.

Walt Disney: One Man's Dream

HS81: The tribute features multiple milestones, inspirations, and facts from the life of Walt Disney. Slow down and read at least three of them.

HS82: Find at least three of the four items on display: Walt's Burbank office, the Abraham Lincoln Audio-Animatronic, an Oscar for *20,000 Leagues Under the Sea*, or the model of Sleeping Beauty Castle.

Fun fact: Walt Disney, the man, is the winner of the most Academy Awards. He has won twenty-two.

HS83: Take the three-question quiz and turn in your answers to a cast member (it will assist you in exploring the pavilion). Bonus points if you get all your questions right.

HS84: Watch the tribute film. Bonus points if you recognize the voice of the narrator.

COMMISSARY LANE

Sci-Fi Dine-In Theater Restaurant

HS85: Tired of sitting at a table and eating. Then eat a meal in your car! Bonus points if you get a milkshake.

HS86: Catch a movie while why you're enjoying your meal. Bonus points if you make it through all the trailers (don't miss *Attack of the 50-Foot Woman*).

HS87: Enjoy a Star Wars Dine-In Galactic Breakfast (try it out on May 4—as in "May the Fourth be with you").

Red Carpet Dreams

HS88: Get a unique picture of Mickey as the sorcerer's apprentice or Minnie as a tinsel-town starlet.

HS89: During your time on the red carpet (also known as the queue), check out the movie posters starring Mickey, Minnie, and their friends. Bonus points if you find the poster that also has the Three Caballeros (Donald, Jose, and Panchito) on it as a shout-out to the Mexico Pavilion at Epcot).

Fun fact: Disney artist Lon Smart designed the posters using classic Hollywood style. If you watch carefully, you will be able to see a bit of animation in each poster.

SUNSET BOULEVARD

HS90: Sunset Boulevard eateries have a shout-out to four different distinct locations (one is an island). Find at least three of the four (cities/islands) that are part of the food stand names.

HS91: At Rosie's All American Café soldier (named after Rosie the Riveter from World War II), find at least three signs featuring Disney characters in battle during the war. Bonus points if you find the Hidden Mickey behind the counter. Hint: Focus on the welding gauge.

HS92: Find the window art (Muscle Beach Bodyguard Service and IBSAD) on the Reel Vogue windows.

Fun fact: Both are shout outs. Muscle Beach Party was a Frankie and Annette movie, and the "We're Standing Behind You" for IBSAD (I be sad) is a reference to the Indiana Jones Epic Stunt Spectacular.

HOLLYWOOD STUDIOS

HS93: Channel your inner villain and check out the scary apothecary. Head into the Beverly Sunset and find the three odes to some of Disney's nastiest villains. Bonus points if you stop by Sweet Spells for a little treat while you're looking.

HS94: Find the 1941 Cadillac. It's hard to miss; just look for the gold car with the unique hood ornament.

HS95: Walt Disney and his brother Roy loved to play polo. Find the photographic tribute to their polo days and the Mickey Mouse short (*Mickey's Polo Team*) that was inspired by it in the Mouse About Town store.

HS96: Review the art-nouveau style of the buildings up and down the boulevard and get to know the actual structures that they represent: Beverly Sunset (Warner Beverly Hills Theater), Legends of Hollywood (Academy Theater, now Academy Cathedral), Once Upon a Time (Carthay Circle Theater), Reel Vogue (35er Bar in Pasadena).

HS97: Find at least three of the gold plated "G Force Records" (in the shape of an actual record) as you cruise the boulevard.

Rock 'n' Roller Coaster

HS98: Countdown with Steven Tyler on Rock 'n' Roller Coaster as you get ready to accelerate from 0 to 57 in the blink of an eye. Bonus points if you can name the only other ride at Walt Disney World that is faster than Rock 'n' Roller Coaster. Hint: It's at Epcot.

Fun fact: Steven Tyler helped open the Rock 'n' Roller Coaster in 1999, but he's been rocking with the band Aerosmith since 1970.

HS99: If you can leave your eyes open long enough, count the number of Hollywood icons that you come across (my personal favorite is the donut). If you catch at least five, your challenge is complete. Bonus points if you've ever lived the Los Angeles freeway experience.

HS100: Hold on to your lunch and complete the only inverted loop/corkscrew in all of Walt Disney World.

HS101: Break up the family (or if everyone else is chicken) and use the single-rider line.

Fun Fact: Did you know the entire ride lasts only 88 seconds.

HS102: As you are waiting to board your limo, figure out the meaning of three of the five license plates.

HS103: As you are boogying along with Aerosmith to get to their concert, figure out the new lyrics that were written for each of their hit songs that play as you enjoy the attraction (for example, "Love in an Elevator" is now "Love in a Roller-Coaster")

Fun Fact: Imagineers had originally thought of using the Rolling Stones instead of Aerosmith.

HS104: Are you boarding Rock 'n' Roller Coaster via FastPass+ or the single-rider line and wearing a Magic Band? If so, find your name in lights (and possibly your hometown).

HS105: Look for the shout-out to the king of rock, Elvis Presley, on the safety signs as guests get ready to board the Rock 'n' Roller Coaster.

HS106: Get your picture with the 40-foot-tall Fender Stratocaster electric guitar. Bonus points if you pose like you're playing air guitar.

Beauty and the Beast—Live on Stage

HS107: Sing along with Lumière and the rest of the staff as they belt out classic Disney hits.

Fun fact: Beauty and the Beast *won an Oscar for Best Original Score.*

HS108: Don't blink. Catch the moment that the Beast transforms back to the Prince.

HS109: Stick around after the show and catch the presentation of the silk rose used during the show to a fortunate guest in the audience. Bonus points if someone in your group gets the rose.

The Twilight Zone Tower of Terror

HS110: Take note of the gardens on the pathway to the entrance of the hotel. Did you see that there is a great deal of overgrowth? If you did, take the challenge points. Bonus points if you come back in the evening and notice special lighting and fog effects in the garden.

Fun fact: The overgrown gardens set the environment of the abandoned hotel and Imagineers used California's Griffith Park and Elysian Park as representative samples.

HS111: Find the signs along the queue directing guests to the bowling green, stables, swimming pool, and tennis courts.

HS112: Upon entering the hotel lobby, find at least three pieces of vintage furniture or sculptures.

Fun fact: Disney purchased antique pieces from the time period from auction houses in Los Angeles.

HS113: Pay attention to the extra details in the queue. Find the issue of *Photoplay* magazine featuring Star Caricatures by Walt Disney (focus on the concierge desk).

HS114: Find at least one item with the Hollywood Tower Hotel "HTH" logo on it.

HS115: In the library room, before or after the video plays, find the channel number that the television is set on. Bonus points if you noticed the brand of the television set.

HS116: True or False. Rod Serling was the host of the original *Twilight Zone* and he also narrates the story on the attraction.

HS117: Watch the introduction video carefully, and find the Mickey Mouse doll.

Fun fact: The doll is representative of a Mickey Mouse doll that one might have in the 1930s.

HS118: Before you board your service elevator, find the Hidden Mickey on the walls of the boiler room (think water stains).

HS119: Smile pretty for the camera (and be sure to strike a pose) before gravity takes over and you begin hurtling toward the lobby.

HS120: You're going to have to be fast with this one. Soak in Hollywood Studios and try to spy a peak of Epcot before you fall.

HS121: True or False. Guests will plummet thirteen stories at a rate of about thirty-nine miles per hour in the service elevator.

HS122: Even though there are no Disney character meet-and-greets with this attraction, get a picture with a Tower of Terror cast member...their costumes are to die for. Bonus points if you get the cast member to smile for your photo.

Fun fact: The Tower of Terror cast member costume is modeled after that of a bellhop from the 1930s. It is one of the most expensive costumes at the parks.

HS123: Search the Tower Hotel Gifts for Talky Tina, a doll featured in the *Twilight Zone* called "Living Doll."

Fun fact: In the episode, Talky Tina terrorized actor Telly Savalas.

Fantasmic!

HS124: Show your Disney side. Attend the show sporting some "Glow with the Show" paraphernalia.

HS125: Mickey is a mouse of many styles. Catch the differences between all three of his costumes and relate them to the appropriate short/movie: *Steamboat Willie*, *Brave Little Tailor*, and *Fantasia*.

HS126: The show is a virtual buffet of villains. Count the Disney villains throughout the show, and name at least six of the eleven. Bonus points if you can match them to the movie in which they appear.

HS127: Two for the price of one. Try out the Fantasmic Dining Package and score VIP seats for the show.

HS128: True or False. When Maleficent changes into dragon form, she is more than 50 feet tall.

HS129: Character Palooza is a meet-and-greet event with multiple characters from Fantasmic that may occur during the show. If it does occur, be one of those guests lucky enough to capture a moment with a few of the less available Disney characters.

Animal Kingdom

OASIS

AK1: Arrive for rope drop (15 minutes before the scheduled opening time should do) and then enjoy short lines, short waits, and low(er) temperatures. Hint: Most guests will head straight to Kilimanjaro Safaris first, but if you zig when they zag, and go to DinoLand, you will basically walk on every ride.

AK2: Try the "secret" entrance/exit located at the Rainforest Café (right next to Oasis). Bonus points if you catch a meal and go back into the park through the same entrance.

AK3: The wilderness must be explored. Tackle the self-guided tours and unique missions and earn at least five Wilderness Explorer badges. Bonus points if you earn at least ten badges.

AK4: Channel your inner veterinarian. Take the Backstage Tales tour to find out how the animals are cared for (food, housing, etc).

AK5: Locate a non-wooden bench anywhere in the park and have a seat.

Fun fact: The benches are made out of recycled milk jugs.

AK6: Welcome to the jungle...or the Oasis. Find at least three of the following five animals in their exhibit: barbirusa, macaw, rhinoceros iguana, spoonbill, wallaby.

AK7: Find the animal prints and leaves along the path.

AK8: Explore the Oasis area on your way out of the Animal Kingdom. Take the opposite trail you entered through, or loop around and do both trails.

DISCOVERY ISLAND

AK9: Examine everything closely. Find at least thirty animals carved into the Tree of Life. Be sure you look at the tree and at the roots. Bonus points if you find more than sixty animals.

Fun Fact: There are 366 animals in total (plus one Hidden Mickey). Give yourself the bonus points if you can find the Hidden Mickey.

AK10: True or False. The Tree of Life is a real tree that Disney horticulturists grew from a seedling.

AK11: Venture down the Tree of Life garden pathway and explore carvings from multiple angles and vantage points. Bonus points if you come across the kangaroo habitat during your journey.

AK12: Beat the heat and meet the main mouse. Head to the Adventurers Outpost and get a picture with Safari Mickey and Minnie (all from the comfort of an air-conditioned indoor getaway). Bonus points if you check out the pictures and keepsakes in the queue area.

AK13: Head to Tiffins restaurant to explore the travel-inspired artwork that celebrates the various different lands that guests may experience around the Animal Kingdom. Bonus points if you find the prayer flags blowing in the wind (reminiscent of Nepal).

AK14: Even the snack kiosks are themed. Find the four themed safari carts on Caravan Road, and check out their unique designs (smiling crocodile, feeding ground, eight spoon café, and terra treats).

AK15: Report to Creature Comforts and find the African warrior shield lights (be sure to check out the octagon-shaped façade before you enter).

AK16: Check out Island Mercantile and look for the magnificently carved animals on and around the building. Find at least five to complete the challenge.

AK17: Locate the columns at the Discovery Trading Company that double as totem poles.

Fun fact: Each of the four totem poles have animals represented that are native to areas in the north, south, east, and west.

AK18: Get a picture with one of the harder-to-find characters at Walt Disney World like Baloo, King Louie, Flik, and Doug. Bonus points if you head to Tusker House for the buffet and character meet-and-greet.

AK19: Let the rhythm get you while you laugh, sing, and dance the night away at the Discovery Island Carnivale.

AK20: Capture the nightly awakening of the Tree of Life and the fireflies bringing different animals to life.

AK21: Take a journey filled with lanterns and spirit animals along the Discovery River lagoon. Join Asma and Aditya and catch the Rivers of Light show.

Fun fact: Asma (limitless) is the human embodiment of water, and Aditya (light and sun) is the embodiment of fire and light.

It's Tough to Be a Bug

AK22: As you wait for your bugtastic show to begin, preview the multitude of theater posters starring bugs (Beauty and the Bees, A Cockroach Line, etc.). Check out five to complete the challenge.

AK23: Snap a picture of your group wearing their "bug eye" glasses.

AK24: Catch all of the special sense effects during the show: blowing air, water shooting, stingers, and movement underneath you. Bonus points if you can find where the Imagineers hid the special-effect triggers.

AK25: Don't scream when you are asked to remain seated while the lice, bed bugs, maggots, and cockroaches exit.

AK26: Upon completion of the show, catch the lighting of the EXIT signs…by what appear to be fireflies.

AFRICA

AK27: Find DiVine on the path between Africa and Asia. Look carefully—she blends in with the foliage.

Fun Fact: DiVine appears on stilts and is decorated like a vine come to life.

AK28: Find the Hidden Mickey of pebbles and stone surrounding a manhole cover on the streets of Africa. Bonus points if you notice three different animal prints while you are searching.

AK29: Head to Zuri's Sweets and review the unique and theme-related treats, then try one of them.

AK30: Check out the African-oriented items in either Ziwani Traders or the Mombasa Marketplace for a one-of-a-kind shopping experience. Bonus points if you check out both.

AK31: Tackle the Wild Africa Trek on a three-hour guided hike of the Harambe Reserve area of Kilimanjaro Safaris. Bonus points if you don't fall off the rope bridge over the crocodiles.

AK32: Give Swahili a chance and greet a cast member with a hearty Jambo (hello).

AK33: In Harambe, review the architecture created at the Tamu Tamu and find the eighteenth-century plaster carvings in the courtyard.

AK34: It's true, sooner or later, the rhythm is going to get you. Head to the Dawa bar and catch the beat of the Congo from the Tam Tam Drummers. Bonus points if you let loose and join in and dance. Double bonus points if you enjoy a bit of dawa (magic potion) at the Dawa Bar while you enjoy the show.

AK35: Complete the Gorilla Falls Exploration Trail. Check out the amazing gorilla habitat and the beautifully detailed scenery throughout the trail. Catch it before you hop on Kilimanjaro Safaris or right afterward. Be sure you catch Timon's relatives, the meerkats, while you're touring.

Kilimanjaro Safaris

AK36: During your two-week safari in the Harambe Reserve (it's actually only 20 minutes or so), find the Hidden Mickey in Kilimanjaro Safaris. Hint: Pay close attention when you get to the flamingos.

AK37: Capture a lion on top of "Pride Rock" during your tour.

Fun fact: Disney placed air conditioning and heat on the stone perch to keep the lions on display.

AK38: Bring the adventure up close. Take a pair of binoculars on the safari with you.

AK39: Get photos (or video) of at least five animals on your safari adventure. Try to sit on the left or right side to get the best shots (or in the middle so you have both sides covered better). If you have one, wear the camera strap around your wrist or neck.

AK40: There are thirty-four different animal species roaming the wildlife reserve. See if you can spot at least twenty of them (use the animal key located behind/above the driver to help you track your progress). Bonus points if you locate thirty different animals.

AK41: When you happen upon the African elephant habitat, locate the secluded pond built specifically for the baby elephants to learn to swim. If you can't find it, ask your driver. Either way, take the points.

Fun fact: There have been at least four baby elephants born at the Animal Kingdom.

AK42: True or False. The baobab trees (look like they are upside down with bare branches) that you find throughout your safari are real

Fun fact: The baobab tree near the Tusker House is real.

AK43: Experience the slight free-fall sensation when your safari truck crosses the dilapidated-looking bridge.

AK44: Find the black vultures located on the plains.

Fun fact: These sneaky birds are not part of the Kilimanjaro Safaris attraction. They are native to Florida.

AK45: Toward the end of the day, keep an ear out for the animals to be called in for supper. Triangles, metal bars, drums, whistles, and cowbells are just a few of the instruments used. Catch two or more of these sounds to complete the challenge.

AK46: Your driver has a plethora of information, and only so much time to share it. Think of a question, and ask your driver. It can be as simple as, "Which animal is your personal favorite?"

AK47: Examine the muddy roads. Did you notice the Disney Imagineers went out of their way to make the concrete look like mud through coloring, tire imprints, and debris? If so, give yourself the points.

AK48: Look for the unique ways that Disney is able to present the animals in their natural habitat while making it appear as if the animals are free to roam from one area to another. Take the points if you find two examples. Hint: Look for chains on the road or a hints of a "pit" space (the lions have a pit that is 18 feet deep and 21 feet wide).

AK49: Find out if the lion actually sleeps at night. Take a safari trip in the evening and compare it to your daytime adventure.

Festival of the Lion King

AK50: Listen carefully as the hosts (Kibbi, Kiume, Nakawa, and Zawadi) introduce themselves and match their names with the meaning (gift, handsome, princess, strength) to complete the challenge.

AK51: Sing along with Simba, Timon, Pumba, and the Lion King gang at the Festival of the Lion King show. Bonus points if you get to sit in the lion section...work on your ROAR.

AK52: Show your section pride and either roar (lion), grunt (warthog), bah (giraffe), or trumpet (elephants) to show your animal pride. Bonus points if you've sat in all four sections at one time or another.

AK53: The show is full of various characters (human and animal). Find three different tribal robes on display during the performance.

Fun fact: There are approximately 136 costumes worn during the show.

AK54: True or False. The Simba puppet is twelve feet tall.

Gorilla Falls Exploration Trail

AK55: Walk the Gorilla Falls Exploration Trail. Check out the amazing gorilla habitat and the beautifully detailed scenery throughout the trail. Catch it before you hop on Kilimanjaro Safaris or right afterwards.

AK56: Find Timon's relatives, the meerkats, during your tour of the trail.

AK57: Find at least three different types of birds during your trek (use the Bird Spotting Guide to help).

AK58: Find the rock structure that resembles Jafar from *Aladdin* while you are on the trial.

AK59: Don't be shy. Engage a Cast Member during your tour (ask about an animal, bird, or plant).

AK60: Earn three of the five Wilderness Explorer badges available. Bonus points if you earn all five (especially if you imitate a gorilla to a cast member).

AK61: Find the skeleton heads of an okai and a firaffe.

AK62: Find the hippopotamus from both the underwater and aerial vantage points. Bonus points if you see the hippo actively swimming.

RAFIKI'S PLANET WATCH

AK63: Ready for a hands-on encounter with some animals? No, not the lions. Head over to the Affection Section and pet the animal of your choice (goats, sheep, and donkeys). Bonus points if you talk to the animals in their native language (oink, bah, etc.). More bonus points if you wash your hands afterward.

ANIMAL KINGDOM   107

AK64: Complete the Habitat Habit adventure trek.

Wildlife Express Train

AK65: Examine the intricacies of this simple train. Find the luggage (look up) and the large antlers (look at the front of the train).

AK66: During your seven-minute journey, find the animal housing shelters along the train tracks. Bonus points if you catch a glimpse of an animal or hear one being called into its stall.

AK67: True or False. The Wildlife Express Train adventure is longer in length than the Walt Disney World Railroad located at the Magic Kingdom.

Conservation Station

AK68: Upon entering Conservation Station, find the large mural with approximately 600 animals highlighted. There are numerous Hidden Mickeys located throughout the mural (embedded in the animals). Find at least one of them.

AK69: Watch an animal being cared for at the veterinary treatment room. Bonus points if you're there during a surgery.

AK70: Join Grandma Willow and take in the Song of the Rainforest.

AK71: Use your trip to the Conservation Station as a learning experience. Take an up-close look at an animal and watch an Animal Encounters stage show.

AK72: Get a picture with Rafiki. Bonus points if you see Chip and Dale or Doc McStuffins.

AK73: Take a backstage tour and get an animal's-eye view of its habitat.

AK74: Creepy, crawlies bring you down? No problem—there's a window pane separation. Find the snakes, millipedes, and tarantulas.

ASIA

AK75: Learn some Indian dance moves. Join in on the street party and shake your groove thing with DJ Anaan at the Festival of All Seasons.

Fun fact: The music is a mixture of Punjabi and Western pop.

AK76: Report to the Serka Zong Bazaar and experience the Himalayan- (and Yeti-) themed atmosphere.

AK77: Find the heavily decorated (and themed) Anandapur bus and check out the homage to Anandapur's adventures, history, and wildlife depicted on panels along the side. Bonus points if you get a soft-serve ice cream or a float.

AK78: Find the utility pole that uses a Coke bottle for insulation.

AK79: Get transported halfway around the world and enjoy Asian-fusion cuisine at Yak & Yeti.

AK80: Catch the musical stylings of Chakrandi and get introduced to the sitar and the table. Bonus points if you can tell which instrument is which. Hint: the sitar has strings.

AK81: Welcome to the Tibetan village. Find two Yeti totems located there. Bonus points if you find a flier announcing the presence of the Yeti.

AK82: Pay homage to the Forbidden Mountain before you approach the attraction. Stop by the shrine with the bronze sculpture and snap a picture. It may be the last one of you and your party.

ANIMAL KINGDOM

Expedition Everest

AK83: Welcome to the entrance of Forbidden Mountain. See how you measure up and find the sign stating that "you must be one Yeti foot tall to ride."

AK84: Find the Ye-Tea (a yeti pun) in the Expedition Everest queue.

AK85: Speed up your quest to ride Expedition Everest and hop in the single-rider line. Try the queue out at least once, though—it's amazing.

AK86: Pay close attention as you make your way through the queue. Find at least three of the five attraction themed shout-outs: Royal Anandapur Tea Company processing lamps (to dry out the tea leaves), permit office, Yeti shrine, Tashi's Trek and Tongba Shop (for supplies), and museum dedicated to a Yeti.

AK87: While waiting to board your locomotive, catch the steam rising as the train enters the station.

Fun fact: The train doesn't actually blow off the steam; it is released by steam vents underneath the station.

AK88: Upon your descent up Forbidden Mountain, find the Yeti footprints in the snow before you reach the mountainside.

AK89: Throw your hands in the air as you experience Forbidden Mountain backwards. Bonus points if you throw your hands up when you make your final plunge down the mountain.

AK90: True or False. The Yeti you experience inside Forbidden Mountain is moving.

Fun fact: The Yeti is covered in three tons of different fur.

AK91: Upon your exit, find the Tibetan mani wall (in the form of multiple stone tablets).

Fun fact: Mani are tablets that have been inscribed with prayers.

Flights of Wonder

AK92: Groucho, the singing parrot...you heard that right. Catch Groucho in full song during the show.

Fun fact: Groucho was named World's Best Singing Parrot and has appeared on The Tonight Show and The Ellen DeGeneres Show.

AK93: Turn around and watch two of the birds fly in from the back of the Caravan Stage amphitheater. Bonus points if one of the bird flies directly over your head (or if you can feel the breeze as it does).

AK94: Volunteer to be part of the show. Offer to hold a one dollar bill for the bird to swoop over to you and collect it (don't worry, the bird will also return your money). Bonus points if you are selected.

AK95: Confused about how the birds know what to do and when to do it? Watch the bird trainers closely as they use audio and visual cues to spark the birds into action.

Fun fact: The birds are not performing tricks during this show. The bird's actions throughout the show generally mimic what one would find in the wild.

AK96: Hang around after the show and speak with Guana Joe and the other trainers. Bonus points if you check out the masterful architecture of the sets that are themed after the Himalayan region of India.

Kali River Rapids

AK97: Play it smart and leave your valuables in a storage locker at the entrance (first 80 minutes are free).

ANIMAL KINGDOM

AK98: Find the office of Manehsa Gurung, the proprietor of the Kali River Rapids Company.

AK99: The attention to detail throughout the line is meant to entertain guests and provide a feel for the Asian culture. Find at least three of the five references to Asian culture while you're in line: native flags, prayer shrine, hand-painted murals, feline statues, and sandals.

Fun fact: The sandals are outside the palace because it is customary to remove your shoes prior to entering a holy area such as temple.

AK100: As you wind your way through the queue, find the paddles adorning the walls from past rafters and read them for a good laugh. Bonus points if you find the paddle that reads "a crocodile ate my paddle."

AK101: Yes, even the rafts have uniquely themed names. Review the names (odes to various areas of Asia) of the rafts as they enter and depart the queue area (or on the raft disposition board). Bonus points if you find the one named after Baloo from *The Jungle Book*.

AK102: Chances are pretty good you are going to get wet. During your ninety-foot ascent up the conveyor belt, pick one of the twelve passengers on your raft as the "most likely to get soaked." You can pick yourself if you are feeling lucky.

AK103: After selecting your winner, take the scent challenge. Catch the aroma of jasmine in the mist as you continue to climb up the incline.

AK104: Later, sniff out the odor of smoke as you come across the logging camp.

Fun fact: Guests used to be able to witness a fire-like effect in the logging section of the attraction.

AK105: True or False. they are serious when they state that "You will get wet. You MIGHT get soaked." There are approximately 150,000 gallons of water to contend with during your rafting experience.

AK106: Find and get squirted by the ornate elephant or the golden cobra.

AK107: Survive the final drop without getting wet. But take the bonus points if you are the winner of the "wettest rafter" contest. Double bonus points if you make it through the entire journey without a drop on you (mist doesn't count).

AK108: On your way out of Kali River Rapids, find the green button that allows guests to shower water down on the rafters and press it. Bonus points if you hit your target (rafters).

Maharajah Jungle Trek

AK109: The attention to detail along the trek is astounding. Find the newspapers from Anandapur on the buildings as you enter.

Fun fact: Anandapur is the fictional village represented and the newspapers lining the buildings are used for insulation.

AK110: Read the Anandapur Royal Forest sign to get the backstory created by Disney Imagineers.

AK111: Find the murals lining the worn walls along the trek and try to decipher the story.

AK112: Find the Nepalese-inspired monument tower. Hint: Check out the gibbon monkey habitat.

AK113: There are multiple small wooden structures and signs littered throughout the trail with artwork depicting the animals in the habitat. Find at least three of these signs to complete the challenge.

ANIMAL KINGDOM

AK114: Pick up a souvenir guide map and follow along as you trek through the jungle.

AK115: Get face to face with the tigers. Hint: The tigers are most active in the morning, but if you catch them about a half hour prior to the trail closing, you may find them pacing near the fountains as they wait for their dinner. Bonus points if you get one to look you in the eye. Bonus points if you catch one playing in the pond (climb the bridge for the best view).

AK116: Review the pictures of bats dwelling in caves in Asia. Bonus points if you recognize Disney Imagineer Joe Rhode in one of the photos (he helped developed the Maharajah Jungle Trek).

DINOLAND, U.S.A.

AK117: Catch the plants and animals that have survived through the years by completing a lap around the Cretaceous Trail. Bonus points for spotting dinosaur footprints.

AK118: True or False. The brachiosaurus that you encounter after crossing over Oldengate Bridge isn't an inch more thirty-five feet tall.

AK119: Find the skeleton of the tyrannosaurus rex, Dino-Sue, and get your picture with her.

Fun fact: Dino-Sue is a replica of the original fossils found by Susan Hendrickson in the Black Hills of South Dakota.

AK120: Give at least one of the midway games a go at Fossil Fun Games. Bonus points if you take a prehistoric prize home with you.

AK121: Find the icon of DinoLand, USA, the cementosaurus (he's hard to miss, but if you are at a loss, ask a cast member).

AK122: Find the Mr. Potato Head in Chester & Hester's Dinosaur Treasures shop. Hint: Think Godzilla. Bonus points for exploring the walls and ceiling of the world's best road-side tacky souvenir store.

AK123: Find the hilarious billboards promoting Chester & Hester's Dinosaur Treasures.

AK124: Head over to Restaurantosaurus and find the "I ARE SMART" sign on the outside of the silver trailer. Figure out the anagram that it stands for. Bonus points if you walk around the various rooms of the restaurant and find three pieces of dinosaur memorabilia left behind by student paleontologists.

The Boneyard

AK125: Plenty to do for any young guests in your party. Watch your child tackle the Boneyard. If you are without a child, drop by and check out the dino-themed playground and take a close look at what is being uncovered in the sandbox.

DINOSAUR

AK126: True or False. The breed of dinosaur that you are searching for, the iguanadon, is the same breed of the main character, Aladar, from the 2000 Disney movie *Dinosaur*.

AK127: While waiting to load into your ride vehicle for DINOSAUR, find the red, white, and yellow pipes. Figure out what the chemical names on the pipes stand for.

Fun fact: DINOSAUR (or Countdown to Extinction as it used to be called) was originally sponsored by McDonald's. That's also a clue to help you figure out what those chemical names stand for.

AK128: Uncover the name pun on DINOSAUR. Hint: It is one of the doctors.

AK129: While in the loading area, find the sector shout-out on the wall that reads: Sector CTX-WDW-AK98 and decipher what it means.

AK130: Non-fossilized dinosaurs are plentiful here. Find at least five as you trek through time.

AK131: Even though there's no steering wheel, score a front-row driver-side seat for your journey.

AK132: The smoke effect throughout the ride is a major part of the attraction. Figure out where the Imagineers ported the smoke in to the attraction.

AK133: Guests may find themselves on the menu in the world of dinosaurs. Your challenge is to not scream when confronted with the carnotaurus (smile pretty, though; it's a photo moment).

TriceraTop Spin

AK134: Work in tandem in your four-person dinosaur and bob up and down (front controls) and forward and back (back controls).

AK135: Keep your eye on crown in the epicenter of the attraction and catch a friendly prehistoric visitor making an appearance.

Primeval Whirl

AK136: Find at least two cartoon-like dinosaurs and two meteors while blasting through time.

AK137: Since your ride vehicle is free spinning, no two rides are the same. Make your ride even more memorable and keep your hands up for all the dips and dives that you experience.

Finding Nemo—The Musical

AK138: While you are waiting to enter the theater, review the multiple messages left behind from the cast of *Finding Nemo* (Bruce, Dory, Squirt).

AK139: Head into the Big Blue, but be sure you have tissues. Laugh and cry with Marlin, Dory, and the gang. Bonus points if you catch one of the bubbles.

AK140: Take a close look around the theater and determine how Disney Imagineers pulled off the underwater effects using lighting, props, and projections.

AK141: Belt out a few choruses of "Big Blue World" as you depart the theater.

Fun fact: The same composers (Robert Lopez and Kristen Anderson-Lopez) that wrote the songs for Finding Nemo later produced the music for Frozen.

PANDORA: THE WORLD OF AVATAR

AK142: When in Pandora, do as the Na'vi do Learn a bit of the native language and greet a cast member with "kaltxi" (hello).

AK143: Engage an ACE expert and ask about the bioluminescent brilliance that is found throughout Pandora. Bonus points if you can get a plant to glow during the daytime. Hint: Block its light.

AK144: Hike underneath the Floating Mountains and explore the intricate details.

Fun fact: The Floating Mountains are able to defy gravity because of unobtanium below and within the mountains, creating a repelling affect.

AK145: Share your energy. Find a Flaska Reclinata plant and set your hand on its side. Take the challenge

ANIMAL KINGDOM

points if the surface glowed and you exchanged energy with the plant.

AK146: Find at least three separate waterfalls and three unique lamps featured throughout Pandora.

AK147: Listen for special sounds throughout the fields of heliocrdian. If you hear the hexapede (a mix of llama and dragon), take the points. Bonus points if you find a helicoradian plant (orange, single-leaf plant) that recoils into the ground if you touch it.

AK148: Find the carnivorous challis plant while you are exploring, but be sure to keep your distance.

AK149: Find the spiny whip and figure out what birds use it for. Ask a naturalist if you can't.

AK150: Life on Pandora isn't all banshees, flora, and fauna. Report to Pongu Pongu (party, party) and unwind with a unique Na'vi-inspired drink.

AK151: Check-in to the Quonset-hut and try a little Na'vi fine dining at Satu'li Canteen. Bonus points if you explore the Na'vi art adorning the walls.

AK152: Find the goblin thistle (also known as the thousand berry tree) and explore its twisting and bountiful growth.

AK153: Pandora is rich with one-of-a-kind plants. Find the bladder polyp (which resembles a blue slug).

Fun fact: The polyp pulls salt from the soil and apparently tastes like a pickle from earth (but don't try to bite one).

AK154: Head to Windtraders and meet your banshee. Take the points if you connect with one. Bonus points if you get a Na'vi action figure made in your likeness.

AK155: As awesome as Pandora is by day, the extra magic begins as the sun sets. Explore Pandora at night and rediscover the bioluminescent plants in all of their glory.

AK156: Don't just focus on the plants, though. Look down and discover the intricacies of the sacred Na'vi ground that you are traversing at night.

AK157: Integrate into the Na'vi culture on the east side of the Valley of Mo'ara and get your face painted Na'vi style at the Colors of Mo'ara.

AK158: Activate plants (and by activate, I mean make them spit water at you) with a flick of your wrist. Bonus points if you get hit with the water.

AK159: Pandora wasn't always peaceful. Find the Amplified Mobility Platform (amp suit).

AK160: Find the dog tags of guests who have undergone the Na'vi-human hybrid processing (head toward Windtraders).

AK161: Take note of the sounds that you hear during the day, and revisit Pandora in the evening. Do you hear different sounds (for example, scavenging-type animals during the day versus predator-type animals during the night)? If so, take the challenge points.

AK162: On your way out, give a hardy "eywa ngahu" (goodbye) to an ACE cast member.

Avatar Flight of Passage

AK163: During your third-of-a-mile queue trek to your banshee, find four of the following: bladder polyp (looks like a large slug), palm tree, waterfall, a vine that makes it from the ground to the top of a mountain, hieroglyphics of a banshee, or hand prints.

AK164: While meandering through the Valley of Mo'ara on the way to your flight of fancy, capture a picture of the impressive forced-perspective mountain range with waterfalls (try to determine which one isn't real).

AK165: Find the Na'vi handprint with the human handprint on top of it in the caves. Bonus points if you find the Na'vi handprint with four fingers (and a thumb).

Fun fact: Na'vi actually only have three fingers and a thumb, but the avatar Na'vi have four fingers and a thumb due to the human DNA.

AK166: Once you exit the bunker section of the queue, find the rusty pipe that is being reclaimed by the jungle of Pandora. Bonus points if you hear a creature scampering inside the pipe.

AK167: What's the name of the xenobiologist you see during the pre-show?

AK168: Pay close attention to the screen as they scan your body for Pandoran micro parasites. If you're contaminated, take the challenge points. Bonus points if you survive the decontamination process.

AK169: Disney Imagineers stepped up their game to mimic the sensation of flight. Identify the following aspects of flight while you soar on your banshee: changes in air density, banking, crosswind, curving, and swooping.

AK170: Flying can wear a banshee out. Feel the labored breathing of your banshee as it takes a brief respite from flying.

Na'vi River Journey

AK171: The Kaspavan River is rich with life, so find at least five of these seven: multi-colored cave mushrooms, stalactite, a Na'vi warrior, spider spores, a glowing flora (looks like a chandelier), and bioluminescent flowers.

AK172: Look overhead during your journey and find a creature playing in the giant leaves.

AK173: Pick out three distinct animal/creature sounds as you venture down river in your reed boat.

AK174: All paths lead to the Shaman. Find at least two native animals and the tribe all venturing toward the lyrical singing of the Shaman. Bonus points if you noticed that all life you experience while you're on your journey is traveling in the same direction.

AK175: Once you come across the nine-foot Shaman of Songs, join the Na'vi in song as you float past.

Fun fact: The Na'vi Shaman of Songs is the most advanced Audio Animatronic ever created by Disney Imagineers.

Walt Disney World Special Events

EPCOT INTERNATIONAL FESTIVAL OF THE ARTS

SE1: Review the artwork of Disney's Herb Ryman, designed the initial concept art that helped secure the financing for Disneyland.

Fun fact: Herb Ryman and Walt Disney spent an entire weekend sketching out the original plans for Disneyland.

SE2: Review the artwork of Disney's Mary Blair, who created concept pieces for Disney-animated films and character design for Disney attractions.

SE3: Catch a musical showcase highlighting Disney's Broadway talent at the America Gardens Theatre.

SE4: Discover a new Disney artist. Bonus points if you happen to purchase a piece of their art.

SE5: Try something new at the Food Studios.

Fun fact: Disney chefs create food so enticing that some guests don't know whether to revere it or consume it.

SE6: Is it real or is it a statue? Check out the living statues display and determine for yourself.

SE7: Learn about the techniques and tricks behind the magic. Attend any one of the many seminars or workshops covering an array of artistic concepts and topics. Bonus points if you attend three or more.

SE8: Immerse yourself in multi-culturalism. Take the five-hour, eleven-country World Showcase: Destinations Discovered tour (be sure to bring your appetite).

EPCOT FLOWER AND GARDEN FESTIVAL

SE9: Amazing Disney character topiaries are sprinkled throughout the park. Find at least six of these topiaries: Mickey Mouse, Donald Duck, Buzz Lightyear, Belle, the Seven Dwarfs (count as one), Lady and the Tramp, Lightning McQueen, Cinderella, Rafiki, or Bambi.

SE10: Walk amongst a thousand converted caterpillars at the butterfly house. Bonus points if you witness a butterfly coming out of its cocoon. More bonus points if a butterfly lands on you.

SE11: Capture a picture of the topiaries with Spaceship Earth in the background.

SE12: Attend at least one of the demonstrations or seminars highlighting the world of gardening.

Fun fact: Over 400 horticulturists set up the festival, and 100 maintain the topiaries.

SE13: Make your way around World Showcase and sample food in at least three different country pavilions.

SE14: Catch an act from yesteryear at the American Gardens Theater during the weekend.

SE15: Channel your inner photographer. Capture a shot of the massive floral hillside with the monorail passing by in the background.

SE16: Engage a gardener; they're easy to find—look for them in the floral-themed golf carts.

SE17: Education is everywhere. Check out at least three of the stationary exhibits located throughout the park and read the information provided.

SE18: Find Tinker Bell's unique fairy house.

EPCOT'S FOOD AND WINE FESTIVAL

SE19: Experience the French Family Meal Traditions event.

SE20: Attend a one-of-a-kind cheese seminar and learn from the professionals.

SE21: Catch the Chocolate Experience: From Bean to the Bar show and check out the handiwork of the resorts pastry chefs...and get a few samples of chocolate, too.

SE22: Pick a course (at an extra cost) and attend. Seminars change from year to year.

SE23: Catch an act from yesteryear at the American Gardens Theater during the evening. Bonus points if it's an 80s band or performer. Double bonus points if you participate in "Eat to the Beat" and enjoy some dinner while grooving to the oldies.

SE24: Wine not your drink of choice? Venture into the world of craft beer and sample a few brews.

SE25: The festival is known for food from around the world (not just the eleven countries presented in the World Showcase). Pick three different locations to try something new.

SE26: Venture out of Epcot to a few of the resorts or Disney Springs to attend at least two other Food and Wine Festival events.

MICKEY'S NOT-SO-SCARY HALLOWEEN PARTY

SE27: Take advantage of the extra three hours you get with your special-event ticket and arrive at the park before the party starts (it doesn't start until 7pm, but you can enter the Magic Kingdom at 4pm).

SE28: Wear your favorite costume to celebrate the Halloween party in style. Be sure you're familiar with Disney's guidelines for what you can and cannot wear.

SE29: Ask a Disney photographer for a Magic Shot. You might get the Headless Horseman or maybe a resident (or three) from the Haunted Mansion.

SE30: Get a treat or drink that is usually only offered during this special event, like the cupcakes with spiders. Bonus points if your treat comes with a souvenir keepsake (popcorn bucket, cup, etc).

SE31: Catch one of the special shows (they have a tendency to change from year to year) and sing along. Bonus points if you attend the dance party.

SE32: Channel your inner child and relive the glory of years gone by...and yes, if you have children in your party, they are more than welcome to go trick or treating throughout the evening with you. Check your park map for locations. Bonus points if you fill your bucket/bag more than three-fourths full.

SE33: Halloween is always a special night for Disney villains. Have a meet-and-greet with at least three Disney villains on their special night. Bonus points if you get your picture with at least two of them.

SE34: Catch some of your favorite Disney characters in their Halloween costumes. Bonus points if you get a picture with at least two of them.

WALT DISNEY WORLD SPECIAL EVENTS 125

SE35: Get a great viewing spot and take-in Mickey's "Boo-to-You" parade. Listen carefully for the clip clop of the Headless Horseman as he makes his way down the route with his head in his hand.

SE36: Complete your night with a special Halloween-themed fireworks show. Sing along with "Grim Grinning Ghosts" as the night sky comes to life.

MICKEY'S VERY MERRY CHRISTMAS PARTY

SE37: Take advantage of the extra three hours you get with your special-event ticket and arrive at the park before the party starts (it doesn't start until 7pm, but you can enter the Magic Kingdom at 4pm).

SE38: Special event = shorter lines. Challenge your party to ride at least ten attractions in the span of three hours. It can be done!

SE39: Line up for and watch Mickey's Once Upon a Christmastime parade. Keep your eyes peeled for the marching toy soldiers. Bonus points if you watch the parade twice in one evening.

SE40: Kick off the holidays in style with fireworks. Catch the breath-taking Holiday Wishes fireworks display from in front of the castle.

SE41: Get your picture with Santa Claus. Bonus points if you meet Mrs. Claus and get a picture with her, too.

SE42: Mickey's Very Merry Christmas Party can be a "special" character bonanza. Meet-and-greet (and hopefully get a picture) with at least one rare character, such as Scrooge McDuck, all seven dwarfs, and Sandy Claws with Jack Skellington from *A Nightmare Before Christmas*.

SE43: Get a picture with Mickey and Minnie Mouse in their best holiday costumes.

SE44: Find the multiple park locations offering free cookies and hot cocoa, and enjoy a treat. Bonus points if you have to use the hot cocoa to heat up your hands (it can get cold in Florida).

SE45: Capture a snowflake on Main Street. Don't catch it on your tongue, though—that magic snow is foam.

SE46: Purchase a little something to help you remember celebrating Christmas at the Magic Kingdom.

RUNDISNEY

SE47: Not really sure how to start, but want to complete a lengthy race? Check out runDisney's website and complete one of Jeff Galloway's running programs.

SE48: Attend a runDisney Health & Fitness Expo before your run. Bonus points if you score a pair of Disney-themed running shoes.

SE49: Sport a Disney costume for the run. Bonus points if you coordinate a costume with a friend (or team).

SE50: Not a runner, but want to cheer on the masses? Find a spot on the race route and lift the spirits of the participants as they pass by.

SE51: Get a picture taken with at least two Disney characters during your run.

SE52: It doesn't have to be a world-record time; you just need to be persistent to finish this challenge. Complete a race (any length). Bonus points if you complete more than one race in a weekend.

SE53: Congratulations! You've earned your medal. Wear it for the rest of your stay at Walt Disney World.

Walt Disney World Resort Challenge

RES1: Upon arrival at your resort room, tune in and catch the latest Disney park information from Stacy.

RES2: Nothing like hearing Mickey (or one of his friends) first thing in the morning. Set up a character wake-up call for a couple of mornings during your stay.

RES3: Walt Disney World is the most popular honeymoon destination in the world. Find a couple celebrating their nuptials and congratulate them Bonus points if you find a couple wearing honeymoon Mickey and Minnie ears. Double bonus points if you were ever that couple.

RES4: It may be a fairy tale come true for your significant other (or your children). Take a horse-drawn carriage ride either at Fort Wilderness Resort & Campground or at Port Orleans: Riverside.

RES5: There are three different monorail lines (one from the Ticket and Transportation Center (TTC) to the Magic Kingdom, one from the TTC to Epcot, and one that goes from the Magic Kingdom to the resorts). Ride at least two of the different lines during your visit.

Fun fact: The monorail system opened with the Magic Kingdom in 1971, and since then has logged enough miles to travel to the moon and back thirty times.

RES6: Select one of the four golf courses and complete a round. Bonus points if you birdie a hole.

RES7: Celebrate a birthday in style with a customized cake made by Disney (you will have to pre-order).

RES8: Check out an outdoor movie at your Disney resort once the sun goes down.

RES9: If you're staying at a Disney resort, try out a refillable mug.

RES10: Try out an adventure on the Seven Seas Lagoon. Head over to Sammy Duvall's Watersports Centre at the Contemporary Resort. Try out some water skiing, paddle boarding, inner tubing, or parasailing.

RES11: You have your choice of two beautifully maintained miniature golf courses. Play 18 holes at either Fantasia Gardens or Winter Summerland. Bonus points if you try both courses at either location. More bonus points if you get a hole-in-one.

DISNEY'S ALL STAR RESORTS

RES12: Get a picture with one of the giant icons at each of the All Stars. Choose from Disney icons like Sorcerer Mickey, Donald playing tennis, the Three Caballeros, or Pongo and Perdita from *101 Dalmatians*.

RES13: Hit the trails and discover the beauty surrounding the resorts. Complete each of the one-mile trails (walk, jog, run) at the All-Stars.

RES14: Arrange a character wake-up phone call.

DISNEY'S ANIMAL KINGDOM LODGE

RES15: Take advantage of the cultural, heritage, and historical expertise of the cast members and report to the Arusha Rock fire pit to hear an African folk tale.

WALT DISNEY WORLD RESORT CHALLENGE

RES16: Go to one of the savannah viewing areas, day or night, and see what animals you can find. Bonus points if you go after dark and find an animal using night-vision binoculars.

RES17: Check out Jambo House and find the thatched ceilings, brick fireplaces, and African art.

RES18: Shop (or just browse) at the Zawadi Marketplace and find goods (Zulu baskets, beaded gourds, scarves) from Africa.

Fun fact: Disney enlisted researchers to travel to Africa to help determine what items should be displayed.

RES19: Feeling adventurous? Go on a Sunset (Wanyama) Safari from the lodge. Be sure to bring your camera and your appetite (a multi-course meal is provided after the safari).

RES20: Try African cuisine at Boma or Jiko. Bonus points if you get to taste a few samples.

RES21: Try one of the special programs available at the lodge, such as flamingo feedings, cookie decorating, and African crafts.

RES22: Note the similarities of the lobby designs in Animal Kingdom Lodge, Wilderness Lodge, and the Grand Floridian.

Fun fact: All three resorts were designed by architect Peter Dominick.

DISNEY'S ART OF ANIMATION RESORT

RES23: Get your picture taken with a larger-than-life character statue from *Finding Nemo*, *Lion King*, *Cars*, and *The Little Mermaid*. Bonus points if you check out the sketches lining the hallways.

RES24: Experience the underwater music in Big Blue, the largest pool on Walt Disney World property. Bonus points if you play in the Righteous Reef Playground.

RES25: Budding artist in your party? Submit a Disney (or Disney-Pixar) character sketch into the front desk to compete to win the daily honor of best drawing. Bonus points if your sketch is selected as the winner.

RES26: Explore the resort and get immersed in the "little-known" facts about the four films highlighted throughout the resort by reading at least five signs.

DISNEY'S BEACH CLUB RESORT

RES27: Two words: Stormalong Bay. Enjoy an afternoon at one of the top pools on Disney property.

RES28: Compare and contrast the Victorian seaside architecture at the Beach Club, the Yacht Club, and BoardWalk Inn.

Fun fact: All three resorts were designed by architect Robert Stern

RES29: Find the chocolate carousel that is the highlight of the Christmas season at the Beach Club.

DISNEY'S BOARDWALK INN

RES30: Walk/jog/run the Crescent Lake loop at the BoardWalk Inn. Bonus points if you don't stop for a treat afterwards. Double bonus points if you do stop.

RES31: Take the BoardWalk Ballyhoo Guided Tour starting from the Belle Vue Lounge. It starts first thing in the morning, and it's free.

RES32: Enter Epcot through the World Showcase entrance next to the BoardWalk Inn.

RES33: Take the boat to Hollywood Studios. Bonus points if you just take the boat ride for the fun of it.

RES34: Have a free evening and want a little free entertainment? Catch a street performer on the Boardwalk.

RES35: Watch the IllumiNations fireworks at Epcot while sitting on a park bench or on the bridge.

RES36: Or, rent a private pontoon boat to enjoy the IllumiNations show with up to ten of your closest friends.

RES37: Looking for an evening out? Enjoy dueling pianos at Jellyrolls (there is a fee) or dance the night away at the Atlantic Dance Hall (entrance is free). Bonus points if you do both.

RES38: Try out some delicious ice cream at Seashore Sweets. Bonus points if you stroll around the area while eating it.

DISNEY'S CARIBBEAN BEACH RESORT

RES39: Mail a coconut from the Caribben Beach to a friend with whom you want to share the magic. (You can do the same thing from the Polynesian.)

RES40: Stay a night in a pirate-themed bed.

RES41: Lounge in a hammock. Bonus points if you can get in and out without falling to the ground.

RES42: Explore all six of the different islands represented at the resort. Bonus points if you take a dip into each of the different pools.

RES43: Explore the pirate-themed pool, Fuentes del Morro, and find the cannons, go on a lookout, and ride the two waterslides.

RES44: Have your pre-teen take a two-hour Pirate Adventure Cruise escapade in search of pirate treasure (sorry, no parents allowed).

DISNEY'S CONTEMPORARY RESORT

RES45: Catch the monorail from inside the resort. Bonus points if this is your last stop in completing the monorail resort crawl (stopping at each of the resorts connected to the monorail).

RES46: Enjoy a leisurely stroll to the Magic Kingdom. Bonus points if you make this trek back to the Contemporary from the park.

RES47: Have a drink (any type) at the Top of the World Lounge located in Bay Lake Tower. Enjoy it on the outdoor viewing deck (the view is of the Magic Kingdom) The deck is free to anyone until four in the afternoon, but at five, only Disney Vacation Club members using points can enter the deck or lounge.

RES48: Dine at the California Grill and enjoy the Magic Kingdom fireworks, but be sure you make reservations early.

RES49: At the marina, find the nautical flags and figure out what each represents.

RES50: Find the large mural (a few stories high) and locate the five-legged goat.

Fun fact: Disney artist Mary Blair created the mural and purposely included the five-legged goat to signify that nature isn't perfect.

DISNEY'S CORONADO SPRINGS RESORT

RES51: Go for a walk or a run on the mile-long trail around the lake and enjoy the scenery.

RES52: Check out the Mayan Pyramid at the Dig Site Pool, or tackle the Jaguar Slide. Bonus points if you take a dip in the largest hot tub on Walt Disney World property.

RES53: Give yourself some challenge points if you've ever attended a convention or meeting at the resort.

RES54: Find the Three Caballeros topiaries and La Fuenta de Las Palomas (Fountain of the Doves).

DISNEY'S GRAND FLORIDIAN RESORT

RES55: Listen to the lobby pianist. Bonus points if you ride the bird-cage elevator just for fun.

RES56: Try the monorail crawl. Check out three of Disney's deluxe resorts (Grand Floridian, Contemporary, Polynesian) while taking the monorail to each.

RES57: Check out the Disney Wedding Pavilion.

RES58: Watch the Electrical Water Pageant on the Seven Seas Lagoon.

DISNEY'S OLD KEY WEST RESORT

RES59: Take a water taxi to Disney Springs (it's a 20-minute ride).

RES60: Play a friendly game of volleyball, shoot some hoops, or work toward match point with some tennis.

RES61: Head to Old Key West's community hall, 2 Conch Flat, to play some games (ping pong, shuffleboard, pool) or do some crafts.

DISNEY'S POLYNESIAN VILLAGE RESORT

RES62: Take the monorail to or from the resort. Bonus points if you've conquered all three monorail resort stops (Polynesian, Grand Floridian, and the Contemporary) in one day.

RES63: Find the Hidden Mickey in the lobby. Hint: Focus on the glass balls.

RES64: Two heads for one of yours—do you remember Trader Sam from Jungle Cruise? He has had the same deal for many years. Check out Trader Sam's Grog Grotto for some outstanding drinks and eats.

RES65: Gorge on Kona Café's acclaimed comfort meal, Tonga Toast (French sourdough toast stuffed with bananas and covered in cinnamon sugar, with strawberry topping or syrup).

RES66: Hang out at the Lava Pool and enjoy the waterfall, the volcano, and slip slide over 142 feet on the waterslide. If you don't have a bathing suit, or you're just visiting the resort, check out the pool for the points. It's worth the visit. Bonus points if you take your child (toddlers to pre-teens) to Lilo's Playhouse.

RES67: Aloha means hello (and goodbye—it's a very versatile word). Say hello to Disney's Spirit of Aloha Dinner Show and enjoy a tropical luau while watching the performers. Bonus points if you get to show off your hula dancing skills.

RES68: Enjoy the evening breeze from the shore of the Seven Seas Lagoon while either watching the Magic Kingdom fireworks or the nightly Electric Water Pageant. Bonus points if you stick around long enough to watch both.

RES69: Meet Lilo and Stitch at 'Ohana during the morning character meet-and-greet breakfast.

RES70: Catch the evening torch-lighting ceremony.

DISNEY'S POP CENTURY RESORT

RES71: Any gamers in the group? Relive the heydays of the 1980s in the Fast Forward Arcade.

RES72: Take a dip in one of the three uniquely shaped pools. Bonus points if you try all three.

RES73: Walk down memory lane and find a relic (giant icon) that reminds you of your childhood. Bonus points if you go as far back as the 8-Track Cartridge.

DISNEY'S PORT ORLEANS RESORTS

RES74: Sing along with Yehaa Bob (singer, piano player, and comedian) at the River Roost Lounge at Riverside. Bonus points if you become part of the show.

RES75: Find the serpent being ridden by Poseidon at the Doubloon Lagoon at French Quarter. Bonus points if you ride down the serpent's tongue (it's okay, it's a slide).

Fun fact: The serpent's name is Scales.

RES76: The Sassagoula River awaits your arrival. Take a stroll along the river and capture the essence of the antebellum South. Bonus points if you complete the entire two-and-a-half mile journey.

RES77: Journey down the Sassagoula River on a "riverboat" and visit Disney Springs.

RES78: Visit Ol' Man Island and try your hand at fishin'. Bonus points if you catch a bass (or bluegill or catfish).

DISNEY'S SARATOGA SPRINGS RESORT

RES79: Stay in one of the Treehouse Villas.

RES80: Set sail on the high seas and cross Village Lake to Disney Springs.

RES81: Saratoga, New York, is home to a major race track. Find three shout-outs to the world of horse racing (paddock, turf club, etc.).

DISNEY'S WILDERNESS LODGE AND THE CABINS AT FORT WILDERNESS

RES82: Enhance your evening with Chip and Dale. Head over to the Meadow Trading Post for a campfire that includes a sing along and cooking of marshmallows. Bonus points if you don't get messy eating your marshmallows.

RES83: Hit the trail on foot at the Cabins and spot two types of wildlife (deer, ducks, rabbits, armadillos, etc.).

RES84: Go on a fishing excursion (you will have to catch and release) for large-mouth bass. Bonus points if you catch a bass.

RES85: Make Robin Hood proud and win the hand of Maid Marion. Try your hand at archery at the Cabins. Bonus points for hitting the target by the end of the training session. Double bonus points if you place an arrow in the bullseye.

RES86: Vaudeville is not dead. Stomp your feet and clap along at the Western-themed Hoop-Dee-Doo Musical Revue and enjoy buckets of home cooked food served family style.

RES87: Explore Fort Wilderness in the most unique way possible: complete a two-hour Segway tour covering multiple stops (the lodge, the stables, and Bay Lake) and various terrains.

RES88: Take the free one-hour Wonders of the Lodge tour highlighting the design and architecture of the resort. Bonus points if you get to see the Fire Rock Geyser erupt.

RES89: Pull up a chair at the Geyser Point Bar and Grill and unwind at the open-air lounge. Bonus points if you try the bison cheeseburger or the Blue Wilderness drink.

RES90: Experience horses first hand at the Tri-Circle-D Ranch. Bonus points if you go on a hay ride or wagon ride. More bonus points if you go on a trail ride.

DISNEY'S YACHT CLUB

RES91: Check out the globe in the lobby and find the Hidden Mickey. Hint: Focus on the continent of Africa.

RES92: Rent a two- to six- person surrey bike and pedal your way around the Boardwalk. Bonus points if you are the only person in your group pedaling.

RES93: Venture to the top of the tallest waterslide at any of the resorts and glide your way to Stormalong Bay.

BLIZZARD BEACH AND TYPHOON LAGOON

RES94: Complete a lap around a lazy river at either Typhoon Lagoon or Blizzard Beach. Be sure that you check out the theming as you float. Bonus points if you do both lazy rivers.

RES95: Tackle the Sand Pail (soft-serve ice cream with waffle cone, sprinkles, whipped cream, cherry, and cookie pieces all thrown into a sand pail) individually or as a group. Bonus points if you take down the entire bucket with the shovel as your spoon.

RES96: Take some surf lessons at Typhoon Lagoon. Bonus points if you stay on your board for more than five seconds. Double bonus points if you ride a wave all the way into shore.

RES97: Not up for surfing...that's all right. Tame the giant waves sans board at the Typhoon Lagoon Surf Pool. Hint: There are life jackets available for use. Bonus points if you try to do a little body surfing.

RES98: Arrive early and try your luck at getting selected to be the Family of the Day. Win the title of Ski Captain at Blizzard Beach or the Big Kahuna at Typhoon Lagoon and give yourself double the points.

RES99: Tackle the Crush 'n' Gusher at Typhoon Lagoon. This unique water coaster will take you up and down the slide. Bonus points if you do at least two of three courses.

RES100: Time to drop straight down 120 feet at almost 60 miles per hour on Blizzard Beach's Summit Plummet. Bonus points if you don't get a wedgie.

RES101: Family time on the water. Ride the newest water attraction at Typhoon Lagoon, Miss Adventure

Falls. Bonus points for finding Captain Mary Oceaneer's parrot Duncan while riding your raft.

RES102: Participate in the Frozen Summer Games at Blizzard Beach. Go with Team Olaf or Team Kristoff and dominate other guests in Ice Pail Relays, Snowball Toss, Ski Pole Limbo, or Slide Races. Bonus points if you get your picture taken with Kristoff or Olaf after the games.

RES103: Skip the walk and enjoy the unique theming of Blizzard Beach with a scenic chairlift ride to the top of Summit Plummet. Bonus points if you tackle all three slides that the chair lift takes you to (Summit Plummet, Slush Gusher, and Teamboat Springs).

Walt Disney World Snack Challenge

SC1: *Carrot Cake Cookie*. This isn't only first on the snack list because it's alphabetical...it's first in my heart, too.

SC2: *Churro*. Deep-fried piece of heaven with cinnamon.

SC3: *Dole Whip*. Take a piece of the islands with you.

SC4: *Popcorn*. Walt Disney World serves over 275,000 pounds of popcorn in a year...enough to fill Space Mountain. Bonus points if you get a souvenir bucket with your popcorn.

SC5: *Mickey Premium Bar*. Chocolate covering ice cream...on a stick. What's not to love?

SC6: *Mickey Pretzel*. Because everything is better shaped like Mickey.

SC7: *Mini Donuts*. Channel your inner Homer Simpson.

SC8: *Edamame* (that's right, a healthy snack). Had to sneak one healthy snack on here.

SC9: *Cupcakes from Be Our Guest*. Or a cupcake from anywhere on property.

SC10: *The Gray Stuff*. I hear it is delicious.

SC11: *Funnel Cake*. Bonus points if you get a special topping to go along with it.

SC12: *Jungle Juice Slushie*. Better than your local 7-11.

SC13: *Mini Baguette*. Bonus points if you quote the line from *Beauty and the Beast*.

SC14: *Ice Cream*. You pick the flavor and location.

SC15: *Cinnamon Roll*. Report to Gaston's Tavern for one heavenly cinnamon experience.

SC16: *Turkey Leg*. This is actually a meal in itsel. Disney serves more than 1.2 million pounds per year.

Disney Springs Challenge

DS1: Check your receipt after every purchase for a coupon. You've completed the challenge if you get a 20% coupon for any restaurant or retail store.

DS2: Spoil yourself with a dinner and a movie at the AMC Theater. Bonus points if it's a Disney movie.

DS3: Take to the skies on the Characters in Flight balloon and enjoy a birds-eye view of Walt Disney World. Bonus points if you do it during one of the fireworks shows and you can see the fireworks.

Fun fact: Characters in Flight is the world's largest tethered hot air balloon.

DS4: Put on the pedometer of your choice and lace up your walking shoes. The theme parks aren't the only place to walk a lot. Explore each of the four areas of Disney Springs.

Fun fact: There is approximately one mile of walkways.

DS5: Catch the Irish dancers at Raglan Road. Bonus points if anyone in your party joins them on stage.

DS6: Report to the BOATHOUSE marina and check out the Amphicars as they launch from shore into the lake for a twenty-minute tour. Bonus points if you take the tour yourself.

DS7: Take a tour of the BOATHOUSE's fleet of boats on display (there are 19 in all). Bonus points if you stay and have a slice of Gibson's S'mores Baked Alaska (it's huge and feeds four).

DS8: Explore all 13 rooms at the World of Disney. Bonus points if you don't leave with a suitcase full of souvenirs. Double bonus points if you do leave with a suitcase full of souvenirs.

Fun fact: The World of Disney is the largest Disney store in the world.

DS9: Catch a musical act at any of the various venues (Riverboat Square, Sunshine Highline, House of Blues, etc). Bonus points if it is a local high-school act.

DS10: Check out the Marketplace Co-op for the latest Disney merchandise. Bonus points if you get something customized (MagicBand, phone case, etc).

DS11: Venture into Splitsville, lace up your bowling shoes, and enjoy a game of bowling (have a bite to eat while you're at it). Bonus points if anyone in your party gets a turkey (not the food...three strikes in a row).

DS12: Take in the master acrobats at Cirque du Soleil.

DS13: Channel your inner Ricky Ricardo at Bongos Cuban Café. Get a picture of you having a seat on one of the multi-colored bongos at the bar.

DS14: Explore the world of LEGOs at the the LEGO Store. Find two of the unique LEGO sculptures to complete the challenge.

DS15: Visit the Ghiradelli Ice Cream & Chocolate Shop and treat yourself to a snack. Bonus points if you score a free piece of Ghiradelli chocolate.

DS16: Explore the Hangar Bar of Indiana Jones' pilot (and part-time sidekick) Jock Lindsey and find at least three shout-outs to Indy.

DS17: There are multiple ways to get to and from Disney Springs, depending on where you start (car, bus, boat , and on foot). Take at least two of these methods.

DS18: Find one of the two Hidden Mickeys in the mural inside World of Disney. Bonus points if you find both.

DS19: ATMs aren't just for money anymore. Head to Sprinkles and order a cupcake via the ATM.

DS20: Check in at Morimoto Asia and find the stunning twenty-foot glass chandeliers adorning the ceiling. Bonus points if you stick around and check out the exhibition kitchen.

Fun fact: Morimoto Asia is the creation of Masaharu Morimoto of Iron Chef America fame.

Disney Character Challenge

THE MAIN CAST

CC1: *Mickey Mouse*. You will be able to find Mickey in all four of the theme parks. Bonus points if you meet him in all four. Bonus points for every shot you get with Mickey and Minnie.

CC2: *Minnie Mouse*. Mickey's better half can be found in all the theme parks also. Bonus points if you meet her in all four. Bonus points if you are wearing a Mickey Mouse hat (or ears) when you see her.

CC3: *Donald Duck*. Bonus points if you capture him in his large sombrero in the Mexico Pavilion at Epcot.

CC4: *Daisy Duck*. Have a meeting with her and Donald at the same time for some major bonus points.

CC5: *Goofy*. Sometimes he loves to hang out with his pal Pluto. Bonus points if you catch them together. Goofy is also known for his athletic ability. More bonus points if you find him in a sports uniform

CC6: *Pluto*. Bonus points if you get him on his back so you can tickle his belly.

CC7: *Chip and Dale*. Usually you won't find one without the other, but see if you can score a photo op with both at one time.

THE PRINCESSES

CC8: *Snow White*. Bonus points if you can get the ruby red lipstick mark on your forehead. Minus points if you offer her an apple

CC9: *Cinderella*. Catch her and a few other princesses at Cinderella's Royal Table (you'll need a reservation). Bonus points if someone in your party dresses up.

CC10: *Aurora*. Bonus points if you find her in Epcot's France Pavilion and ask her to speak some French.

CC11: *Ariel*. Bonus points if you get one of her in fins and in a dress.

CC12: *Belle*. Bonus points if you get one of her in her village dress and the ball gown dress.

CC13: *Jasmine*. Bonus points if you meet her and Aladdin (or the Genie) at the same time.

CC14: *Pocahontas*. Bonus points if she has an animal with her during the picture.

CC15: *Mulan*. Bonus points if you ask her what Mushu is really like

CC16: *Tiana*. Tiana can be found in the parks, but you get bonus points if you visit her restaurant on the *Disney Wonder* cruise ship. Bonus points if you meet Louis (the alligator) and Tiana at the same time.

CC17: *Rapunzel*. Bonus points if you tell her you love what she has done with her hair.

CC18: *Merida*. Bonus points if anyone in your party has red wavy hair.

CC19: *Anna*. Bonus points if you offer her a sandwich.

CC20: *Queen Elsa*. Bonus points if you get her to tell you to just "Let it go."

CC21: *Elena of Avalor.* Bonus points if you get a picture of Elena holding her sceptre.

CC22: *Moana.* Bonus points if you throw an "I Love You" or "Hang Loose" hand sign during the picture.

THE BEST OF THE REST

CC23: *Aladdin.* Bonus points if you catch him in the Magic Kingdom and at Epcot.

CC24: *Alice.* Wish her a very merry un-birthday and ask to her a tea party. Bonus points if she is teamed up with the White Rabbit or the Mad Hatter

CC25: *Anastasia , Drizella, and Lady Tremaine.* These three generally appear together. Bonus points if you can get Lady Tremaine to crack a smile. More bonus points if you flirt with one of the step-sisters.

CC26: *Baymax.* Bonus points if you get a fist bump.

CC27: *Bert.* Bonus points if you meet him in his Chimney Sweep and Jolly Holiday outfits.

CC28: *Br'er Fox.* Bonus points if either Br'er Rabbit or Br'er Bear are in the picture.

CC29: *Buzz Lightyear.* Bonus points if you point and yell "To infinity, and beyond!" while taking a picture with him.

CC30: *Captain Hook.* Bonus points if you hold your index finger up in the shape of a hook. More bonus points if you ask him how his pet crocodile, Tick Tock, is doing.

CC31: *Cruella De Vil.* Bonus points if you get her to crack her icy exterior.

CC32: *Fairy Godmother.* Bonus points if you get her to lay a spell on you.

CC33: *Gaston*. Bonus points if you challenge him to an arm wrestling or push-up contest. Bonus points if you tell him Belle made the right decision.

CC34: *Genie*. Bonus points if you share your three wishes with him.

CC35: *Green Army Men*. Bonus points if you are wearing any kind of fatigues or Armed Services shirt (Army, Navy, Air Force, Marines).

CC36: *Joy and Sadness*. Bonus points if you act your favorite emotion during a photo op.

CC37: *Mad Hatter*. Bonus points if you know what the 10/6 on his hat means.

CC38: *Mary Poppins*. Bonus points if you get a picture of her in her Jolly Holiday outfit and nanny costume.

CC39: *Mr. Incredible*. Bonus points if you get a picture with him and Mrs. Incredible or Frozone.

CC40: *Olaf*. Bonus points if you get a hug that will melt your heart.

CC41: *Peter Pan*. Bonus points if you get to play Follow the Leader as he heads to his meet-and-greet location. Bonus points if you get to meet Wendy at the same time.

CC42: *Pinocchio*. Bonus points if you sing "I've Got No Strings on Me" when you meet him.

CC43: *Rafiki*. Bonus points if you get Rafiki to act like he is knocking you upside your head.

CC44: *Stitch*. Bonus points for sharing your best Elvis impersonation with Stitch.

CC45: *Tarzan*. Bonus points if you do the Tarzan scream. More bonus points if he does it with you.

CC46: *Tigger*. Bonus points for bouncing up to Tigger.

CC47: *Tinker Bell*. Bonus points if you are the first visitor in line at her meet-and-greet on Main Street, and you get the honor of waking her up.

CC48: *Winnie the Pooh*. Bonus points for acting like you're a little rumbly in your tumbly.

CC49: *Woody*. Bonus points if you catch sight of the name "Andy" on the bottom of his boot.

STAR WARS

CC50: *BB-8*. Bonus points if you ask him how his cousin R2-D2 is doing.

CC51: *Chewbacca*. Bonus points if you wear a Star Wars-themed "Dark Side" character t-shirt to meet him.

CC52: *Kylo Ren*. Bonus points if you ask him how his Father's Day went.

CC53: *Stormtroopers or Captain Phasma*. Bonus points if you get to march with them.

Quiz Answers

If you made it all the way to back of the book to check your answers, then you are truly a Disney Nerd (and I mean that in the most positive way possible). The answers are presented in the order that the question appeared in the book. Just match the challenge number.

MK55: The *Titus*.

MK66: False. The thatched roof only looks real. It is actually made of aluminum strips cut to look like a thatched roof. The aluminum strips serve as a lightning rod to product the attraction.

MK68: Fritz (Germany), Jose (Mexico), Michael (Ireland), Pierre (France).

MK72: 1313 Harbor Blvd, Anaheim, California, is the address for Disneyland. The zip code 71755 is the date that Disneyland opened: July 17, 1955. The actual zip code is 92802.

MK76: The plane is in the Casablanca scene of the recently closed Great Movie Ride in Hollywood Studios.

MK78: Amazon, Congo, Mekong, and Nile.

MK84: True.

MK98: False.

MK112: G. Willikers.

MK119: True—by about five miles per hour.

MK127: Tex Ritter.

MK128: Baby Oscar.

MK130: Tampa.

MK146: False.

MK172: The waltzing ghost couples were created using a theater effect called Pepper's Ghost from the 19th century. The effect illuminates a reflection of the ghost on a pane of glass and makes them look translucent. However, since it is a reflection, everything is turned around and the women appear as if they are leading the men in the waltz.

MK173: Lady Tremaine from *Cinderella* and Maleficent from *Sleeping Beauty*.

MK178: 1787, the year of the Constitutional Convention.

MK182: Morgan Freeman.

MK183: 87; a score equals twenty years.

MK185: He is sitting in a wheelchair. President Roosevelt was paralyzed from the waist down due to polio.

MK189: False.

MK206: True.

MK207: Windows and blocks in the higher areas of the castle were made smaller than those below, thus tricking you into believing they are higher than they really are.

MK222: Pepper's Ghost, using glass and lights to project an image, was used for the Haunted Mansion.

MK238: Disney.

QUIZ ANSWERS

MK241: Haunted Mansion, Under the Sea ~ Journey of the Little Mermaid, and Buzz Lightyear's Space Ranger Spin. Bonus: It's inverted/suspended.

MK246: True.

MK268: Bashful, Doc, Dopey, Happy, Grumpy, Sleepy, and Sneezy.

MK277: True. Ursula measures at 7.5 feet tall and 12 feet wide.

MK285: True, but it's just the spine of the book.

MK294: The one on the left rotates clockwise. It is the only Disney attraction that does not rotate in a counter-clockwise manner.

MK302: True.

MK315: *A Christmas Story*. Bonus: Mel Blanc.

MK327: The Omega track is longer by 10 feet.

MK328: If you guessed twenty-eight miles per hour (or were within 2 MPH), take the points.

MK339: True. Disney uses a technology known as digital puppetry which allows voice actors behind the scene to provide the dialog while the computer generates the monsters' appearance.

MK352: Bonus points: chili hot dog. More bonus points: Journey Into Imagination with Figment (skunk) and It's Tough to Be a Bug (stink bug).

MK353: False. It is 39 inches and is one of the more complex Audio-Animatronics that Disney Imagineers have created.

MK354: Astro Orbiter.

MK356: True. Currently, you'd still have a parking lot that could fit 500 cars in it.

EP8: True. That's approximately 89,000 pounds per foot—it's 180 feet tall.

EP10: Dame Judi Dench. Bonus: "Thank the Phoenicians."

EP18: If you answered false, take the points. The track measures 5,246 feet (just 34 feet short of a mile), making this attraction the longest ride in Walt Disney World.

EP20: True. Up to 150 guests could be enjoying the attraction at one time.

EP35: Bonus: Monsters, Inc. Laugh Factory.

EP58: It's in homage to Epcot opening in 1982.

EP60: True. Mike Brassell provides narration for both attractions.

EP61: True—and the Pirates of the Caribbean, too.

EP64: False. Actually, over 30 tons of produce is grown, and some of it is used on property.

EP67: Kronk from *Emperor's New Groove*.

EP70: True.

EP71: The attraction opened in Epcot on May 5, 2005 (thus 5505).

EP76: Bonus: Dr. Channing (Journey into Imagination), Dr Szalinski (Honey, I Shrunk the Audience), and Dr Brainard (*Flubber*).

EP77: True. Figment became so popular that he is often equated with being the main character associated with Epcot.

EP98: "it's a small world" in the Magic Kingdom.

EP113: True.

QUIZ ANSWERS

EP119: Bonus: twelve = months of the year, and the twelve-year cycle of the Chinese calendar, whereas the four columns represent the four seasons.

EP139: This wall covers the entrance to what was going to be the Rhine River attraction; however, the attraction wasn't built and the area is used for storage.

EP152: The number four is displayed as IIII instead of IV. It is a correct representation for the time period since clock makers would use IIII during colonial times. Bonus: Cinderella Castle.

EP153: Imagineers made the doors and windows taller than usual.

EP180: No lighting is used on any of the pavilion buildings. Norway also stays dark for balance around the showcase.

EP191: True.

EP193: The crossing of the English Channel.

HS18: Dockside Diner.

HS25: False. The giant rolling ball weighs 440 pounds.

HS32: "I've got a bad feeling about this."

HS61: True. The Imagineers designed the size of the items in the room to replicate what life as a toy would feel like for guests; thus, a six-foot guest would feel about fifteen inches tall.

HS69: True.

HS79: True.

HS115: The television is set to channel 13, and the brand of the television is Disney Parks Blog.

HS116: False. Voice actor Mark Silverman performs the narration.

HS121: True, and the drop sequences are randomly generated.

HS128: True.

AK10: False. The Tree of Life is actually an old oil rig that provides the support structure for the tree.

AK42: If you answered false, take the points. The baobab trees on the safari are made of concrete and store feed, lawn mowers, and other things. The ostrich eggs and termite mounds are also concrete.

AK50: Zawadi (gift), Nakawa (handsome), Kibibi (princess), Kiume (strength).

AK54: True.

AK67: False. The Wildlife Express Train track is 1.2 miles in length, and the Walt Disney World Railroad track covers 1.5 miles.

AK90: False. The Audio-Animatronic Yeti currently uses strobe lighting to produce a movement-like effect, earning it the nickname of Disco Yeti.

AK105: True. Seven pumps help move the water to ensure there's not a dry person left.

AK111: Animals and plants lose ground and natural resources to humans, who are punished by the gods for breaking the natural balance of the environment. The humans change their ways and replace a tree for every tree that is cut down. The final mural depicts both animals and humans paying their respects to the tree.

AK118: False. The skeleton of the brachiosaurus is 40 feet in height and is a replica of bones found in Colorado in 1900.

AK124: AIRSTREAM (aluminum trailers with rounded bodies).

QUIZ ANSWERS

AK126: True. The ride was formerly known as Countdown to Extinction, but was renamed in 2000 to match the movie *Dinosaur*. Guests are on a search for an iguanadon which matches the breed of dinosaur that Aladar was from the movie. The dinosaur outside of the attraction is an Iguanadon.

AK127: They are the chemical names for the ingredients in ketchup, mayonnaise, and mustard.

AK129: CTX = Countdown to Extinction, a shout-out to the former name of the attraction, WDW = Walt Disney World, and AK98 = the year 1998, when Animal Kingdom opened.

AK149: Birds like to use it as a bird bath; it collects water.

AK167: Dr. Jackie Ogden. (There really is a Jackie Ogden who used to be the VP of Animal Programs at Animal Kingdom.)

About the Author

William Bragg grew up exactly sixty minutes from Disneyland and began his infatuation with Disney as a toddler. He currently lives with his wife, Jennifer, and two "Disney"-raised kids, Abigail and Landon, in New Braunfels, Texas. William has served in the United States Air Force for the past twenty-four+ years.

His infatuation with Disney has served him well through the years. His loving new wife gladly ventured to Walt Disney World on their honeymoon, his first introduction to the Florida Project. Having been a West Coast Disney fan for most of his life, William was hooked on all the magic that could be found at Disney World. Throughout the past twenty years he has translated his love for Disney into a master's thesis, Disney cruises, and multiple trips to the theme parks on both coasts. Trying to bring a bit of the Disney magic home and wanting to share it with others, William even became an Authorized Disney Vacation Planner for Mickey's Travel agency.

William invests a great deal of his time studying Disney history, business practices, and theme park tales in books (especially books from Theme Park Press). In order to keep up on the latest Disney happenings, he follows WDW Radio, Big Fat Panda, and Tim Tracker (the latter of whom are on You Tube).

About Theme Park Press

Theme Park Press publishes books primarily about the Disney company, its history, culture, films, animation, and theme parks, as well as theme parks in general.

Our authors include noted historians, animators, Imagineers, and experts in the theme park industry.

We also publish many books by first-time authors, with topics ranging from fiction to theme park guides.

And we're always looking for new talent. If you'd like to write for us, or if you're interested in the many other titles in our catalog, please visit:

www.ThemeParkPress.com

....

Theme Park Press Newsletter

Subscribe to our free email newsletter and enjoy:

- ♦ Free book downloads and giveaways
- ♦ Access to excerpts from our many books
- ♦ Announcements of forthcoming releases
- ♦ Exclusive additional content and chapters
- ♦ And more good stuff available nowhere else

To subscribe, visit www.ThemeParkPress.com, or send email to newsletter@themeparkpress.com.

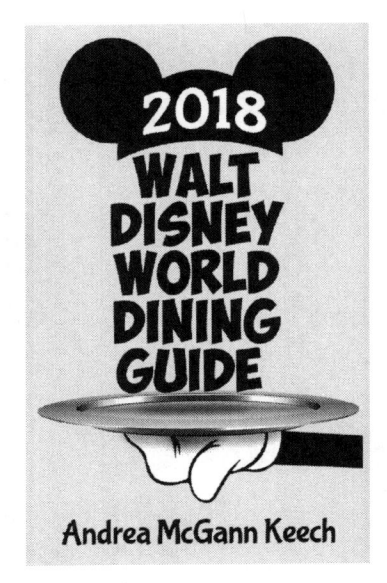

Disney till you're dizzy
VOLUME ONE
1001 FACTS, RUMORS and MYTHS about Walt Disney World

Alexa Erekson

2018 WALT DISNEY WORLD DINING GUIDE

Andrea McGann Keech

THE WALT DISNEY WORLD THAT NEVER WAS
Stories Behind the Amazing Imagineering Dreams That Never Came True

Christopher E. Smith

Walt Disney World for Vampires, Zombies, and Others with Very Special Needs

Dominick Cancilla

Read more about these books and our many other titles at:

www.ThemeParkPress.com

Made in the USA
Lexington, KY
24 April 2018